CHRISTIAN COUNSELING

DR. MAXWELL SHIMBA

Published in Manhattan, New York by Shimba Publishing, LLC.

Scripture quotations are from The New King James Version
Copyright © 1982
Used by permission. All rights reserved.

The Scripture quotation noted KJV is from King James Version of the Bible.

Shimba Publishing LLC

Printed in the United States of America

First Printing Edition 2024

Table of Contents

Introduction

Christian counseling is a form of therapy that incorporates Christian beliefs, values, and practices into the therapeutic process. This distinct approach aims to assist individuals, couples, and families in addressing their problems and challenges in a manner consistent with biblical principles.

Christian counselors are trained professionals who utilize a variety of techniques and approaches grounded in Christian theology and spirituality. They provide services rooted in the Christian faith, seeking to help clients achieve healing and wholeness in their emotional, psychological, relational, and spiritual well-being.

The objectives of Christian counseling include helping clients understand and apply biblical principles to their lives, deepening their relationship with God, and finding practical solutions to their problems. Christian counselors collaborate with clients to explore the root causes of their issues, develop coping skills and strategies, and strengthen their faith and relationship with God.

The origins of Christian counseling date back to the early Christian church, where pastors and spiritual leaders offered guidance and support to their congregations. Over time, the practice has evolved to incorporate modern therapeutic techniques and approaches while maintaining its foundation in Christian principles.

Christian counseling addresses a wide range of issues, such as anxiety, depression, addiction, marital problems, family conflicts, grief, and other mental health concerns. Christian counselors may work in various settings, including private practices, churches, and community-based organizations.

A key principle of Christian counseling is the belief that each person is a unique creation of God with inherent worth and value. Christian counselors view their clients through this perspective and strive to help them understand and embrace their God-given identity and purpose.

Another important principle is the belief that true healing and wholeness come from a deep and abiding relationship with God. Christian counselors assist clients in developing and deepening their relationship with God, providing comfort, strength, and guidance during difficult times.

In Christian counseling, prayer is often used to connect with God and seek His guidance and wisdom. Counselors may also incorporate Scripture reading, meditation, and other spiritual practices to help clients connect with God and seek His will for their lives.

Christian counseling emphasizes the importance of forgiveness and reconciliation. Clients are encouraged to seek forgiveness from God and those they may have hurt and to work towards reconciliation and restoration in their relationships.

Although Christian counseling is rooted in Christian beliefs and values, it is not limited to individuals who identify as Christians. Christian counselors can serve individuals of any faith background or those with no specific religious affiliation but are open to exploring spiritual issues as part of their therapeutic process.

To become a Christian counselor, individuals typically must complete a degree program in counseling or a related field and receive training in Christian theology and spirituality. These programs may include coursework in biblical counseling, Christian psychology, and pastoral counseling.

In summary, Christian counseling is a unique form of therapy that integrates Christian beliefs, values, and practices into the therapeutic process. It helps individuals, couples, and families find healing and wholeness in their emotional, psychological, relational, and spiritual well-being. Christian counselors provide a safe and supportive environment where clients can explore their problems and challenges consistent with biblical principles and seek practical solutions.

Counseling: How to Give Biblical Hope with Practical Help

Giving biblical hope with practical help requires a blend of spiritual insight and practical guidance. Here are effective ways to provide biblical hope with practical help:

1. Start with Prayer: Begin by praying for guidance, wisdom, and discernment as you seek to offer help and hope to others.

2. Listen Attentively: When someone comes to you seeking help, listen attentively to their story, concerns, and needs. Show empathy, compassion, and understanding as you connect with them on a deeper level.

3. Offer Biblical Guidance: Share biblical truths, promises, and principles that bring comfort, encouragement, and hope. Use relevant Scriptures to help them find solace and direction in God's word.

4. Provide Practical Help: Offer practical support that can help them overcome their challenges. This may include referring them to

professional help, providing resources or tools, or offering practical advice or assistance.

5. Show Love and Kindness: Demonstrate care by expressing love, kindness, and compassion. Let them know they are not alone and that you are there to support them.

6. Encourage Faith and Trust: Help them trust in God's goodness, faithfulness, and sovereignty. Encourage them to have faith that God will provide for their needs and that He is working all things together for their good.

By combining biblical hope with practical help, you can help others find strength, comfort, and hope in God's word and in practical ways that address their specific needs and challenges.

"First seek the counsel of The Lord." (1 Kings 22:5)

What is Counseling?

Counseling is the help and hope given by one knowledgeable person to another person or group. It ranges from personal comfort and encouragement to group crisis intervention. Counseling is a form of psychological therapy that involves talking with a trained mental health professional to help address and manage a range of emotional, psychological, and behavioral problems. The goal of counseling is to provide support, guidance, and insight to individuals or groups experiencing challenges or difficulties in their lives.

Counseling can address a wide range of concerns, including anxiety, depression, relationship problems, grief, trauma, addiction, and other mental health issues. It typically involves a series of structured sessions where the counselor and client work together to identify underlying issues, set goals, and develop strategies for managing and coping with these issues.

Counseling sessions may involve various techniques and approaches, including cognitive-behavioral therapy, psychodynamic therapy, humanistic therapy, and others. These techniques help clients gain insight into their thoughts, feelings, and behaviors, develop coping skills, and improve their overall well-being.

Counseling is typically provided by licensed mental health professionals, such as psychologists, licensed clinical social workers, or licensed professional counselors. It may be offered in individual or group settings and can be conducted in person or online. The frequency and duration of counseling sessions vary depending on the client's needs and goals.

What is Christian Counseling?

Christian counseling is an approach to counseling grounded in a biblical worldview, incorporating aspects of modern psychology compatible with that worldview. Christians in the field of psychology, and the roles of counselors and the church, may use Bible-based techniques to accomplish their tasks. Stanton Jones defines it as integrating Christianity and psychology by living out the lordship of Christ over all existence, giving God's true Word its appropriate place of authority in determining beliefs and practices toward reality and academic subject matter ("An Integration View," Psychology & Christianity: Five Views, 2nd ed., IVP Academic, 2010, p. 102).

Christian counseling integrates Christian beliefs, values, and practices into the therapeutic process. It is grounded in the Christian faith and aims to help individuals, couples, and families address their problems and challenges in ways consistent with biblical principles.

Christian counselors use various techniques informed by Christian theology and spirituality, such as prayer, Scripture reading, meditation, and other spiritual practices to help clients connect with God and seek His guidance and wisdom.

The goal of Christian counseling is to help clients find healing and wholeness in their emotional, psychological, relational, and spiritual well-being. Christian counselors work with clients to explore the root causes of their problems, develop coping skills and strategies, and deepen their faith and relationship with God.

Christian counseling can address issues such as anxiety, depression, addiction, marital problems, family conflicts, grief, and other mental health concerns. Christian counselors may work in various settings, including private practices, churches, and community-based organizations.

It is important to note that Christian counseling is not limited to those who identify as Christian. It can be beneficial for individuals of any faith background or those without a specific religious affiliation but who are open to exploring spiritual issues as part of their therapeutic process.

What is the First Commitment a Person Endeavoring to Counsel Should Have?

The first commitment for anyone seeking to counsel should be to inquire for the Word of the Lord (1 Kings 22:5).

For example, Ahab had organized a group of 400 prophets who replaced the prophets of Baal that had been slaughtered after the showdown with Elijah (1 Kings 18). These prophets were called by the king, not by God, making them "yes-men" who told the king what he wanted to hear.

Ahab's prophets, who were prophets of Asherah (1 Kings 18:19), had unanimously given the king a green light to go to war. However, Jehoshaphat wanted a "prophet of the Lord," sensing that Ahab's prophets had a lying spirit (1 Kings 22:23).

If you seek to get to the bottom of an issue, find truth, and know God's thoughts on a situation, it is always best to inquire of the Lord first.

What is the Meaning of Biblical Counseling?

Biblical counseling means relying on the truth from the Word of God to give wise counsel. Christ-centered counseling involves giving advice, encouragement, and hope to others based on biblical truths while relying on Christ to provide the power for change.

- 2 Corinthians 5:17: "If anyone is in Christ, he is a new creation."

- This promise applies to anyone in Christ, regardless of class, race, nationality, language, or intelligence.

- Old things have passed away; behold, all things have become new.

Even after pouring out your heart, time, and effort, some people may not listen to wise counsel and choose the way of the flesh and the world. Don't take it personally. God changes hearts and minds. Your responsibility is to plant the seed of truth and trust the Lord of the harvest to bring the increase.

- Lead an unbeliever into a personal relationship with Jesus.

- Present wisdom from God's Word to enable strugglers to live in victory.

- God's word has the answer for every problem in life. To give godly advice, you must have intimate knowledge of the Scriptures. Truths from the Word of God will bring life and plant the seed of knowledge in the heart of the hearer. The Holy Spirit will speak most loudly the words of God from the Bible.

Why is it Beneficial for the Biblical Counselor to Pray Regularly?

Prayer is essential in Biblical counseling as it ensures the counselor is guided and directed by God in their words and actions. Here are several reasons why it is beneficial for the Biblical counselor to pray regularly:

1. Seek God's Guidance: Prayer is a way to seek God's guidance and wisdom as the counselor works with clients, ensuring they follow God's will and not their own understanding.

2. Connect with God: Prayer deepens the counselor's relationship with God, helping them honor Him in all aspects of their work.

3. Promote Spiritual Growth: Prayer encourages spiritual growth and development in both the counselor and the client, urging clients to seek God's guidance and wisdom in their lives.

4. Foster Empathy and Compassion: Prayer fosters empathy and compassion in the counselor, ensuring they focus on the client's needs and serve them compassionately.

5. Provide Comfort and Support: Prayer provides comfort and support to clients struggling with difficult emotions or circumstances, creating a safe and supportive environment where clients feel heard and understood.

Prayer is vital in Biblical counseling as it ensures the counselor seeks God's guidance and wisdom while promoting spiritual growth, fostering empathy and compassion, and providing comfort and support.

What Should You Do Before Your Counseling Session Starts?

Start by preparing the physical setting by:

a) Providing a private, relaxing place to talk.

b) Eliminating distractions, such as radios, TV, music, other voices, etc.

c) Preventing interruptions by holding phone calls or using a 'Do Not Disturb' sign.

d) Avoiding physical barriers by not sitting behind a desk unless an authoritative tone is needed.

e) Adjusting lighting to reduce glare by adjusting blinds, curtains, or overhead lights.

f) Keeping counseling aids handy, such as a Bible, paper, pens, or referral or resource numbers.

g) Placing facial tissues or drinking water within reach.

Promote personal nonverbal nurturing by smiling or shaking hands upon greeting a person, situating chairs in close proximity, turning your body to face the person, and slanting your body forward to show interest. Nod your head occasionally to show acceptance instead of rejection.

Most people seeking godly advice genuinely want to do the right thing, even if they are deceived by selfish desires. They need reminders of God's grace to help them through difficulty. Avoid making quick judgments about their motives. Only God knows the hearts of men and women, so be gentle and approachable.

When probing for the real problem, use the person's first name several times. To explore the person's past, ask background questions about family, home, school, dating, work, etc. Listen to what is not shared and ask open-ended questions that cannot be answered with a simple yes or no. Explore the impact of significant people in their lives, such as parents, siblings, other relatives, and friends.

We Have All Been Created with Three God-Given
Inner Needs:
a) John 15:12: Love
b) Psalm 57:2: Significance
c) Proverbs 14:26: Security

At the heart of our negative behavior is an attempt to meet our legitimate needs in illegitimate ways. The Bible calls this sin. Proverbs 14:12 says, "There are ways that seem right to men, but in the end, it leads to death." We may be completely sincere about a decision but still be totally wrong. We need to check the Word to ensure we are right. By opening our Bible, reading applicable verses, and rightly dividing and applying them, we will make the right choices.

In Romans 7:24-25, Paul reveals that Jesus Christ our Lord is our ultimate guide and Leader. From the beginning, the Lord planned to meet our deepest needs for:

a) Love: Jeremiah 31:3 - He loves us with an everlasting love.

b) Significance: Jeremiah 29:11 - He knows the plans He has for us, to give us a future and a hope.

c) Security: Hebrews 13:5 - He will never leave or forsake us.

Romans 12:2 says we can be transformed by overcoming negative patterns in our lives by not conforming to this world and by renewing our minds.

The Path to Becoming F-R-E-E:

a) Face the truth of your negative habit: Psalm 139:23

b) Recognize the inner needs you are trying to meet through the negative habit: Psalm 51:6

c) Exchange trying to meet your need by allowing Christ to meet it: Philippians 4:19

d) Experience Christ's inner strength as your source for change: Philippians 4:13

We can all be transformed to be like Christ because, in Colossians 1:27 and John 8:36, the Word of God says, "Christ in you, the hope of glory." He is our hope of freedom, for "if the Son sets you free, you are free indeed."

Our success in counseling comes from knowledge and understanding that God alone can supply through His presence, power, and character reflected in us.

CHAPTER 2

Abortion Recovery: Healing and Restoration After an Abortion Decision

"The Lord is close to the brokenhearted and saves those who are crushed in spirit." (Psalm 34:18)

Healing and restoration after an abortion decision can be a difficult and complex process, but it is possible with the right support and resources. Acknowledge that every person's experience is unique, and there is no one-size-fits-all solution. Here are some general steps to facilitate healing and restoration:

1. Seek Professional Help: Consider seeking the help of a professional counselor or therapist with experience working with individuals who have had an abortion. They can provide a safe, non-judgmental space to explore emotions, process grief, and develop coping skills.

2. Find Support: Connect with others who have had similar experiences. Look for support groups, online forums, or other resources that can provide a sense of community and understanding.

3. Practice Self-Care: Take care of yourself physically, emotionally, and spiritually. Engage in regular exercise, get enough sleep, practice relaxation techniques, and participate in activities that bring joy and fulfillment.

4. Seek Forgiveness and Healing Through Prayer: Many people find comfort and healing through prayer and spiritual practices. Seek forgiveness and healing through the love and grace of God.

5. Take Time to Grieve: Allow yourself time to grieve the loss of the pregnancy and the decision to have an abortion. This process takes time and may involve a range of emotions, such as sadness, guilt, shame, anger, and regret.

6. Reach Out to a Pregnancy Resource Center: Many pregnancy resource centers offer post-abortion support and resources to help with healing and restoration.

Remember that healing and restoration are possible. It may take time, patience, and effort, but with the right support and resources, finding hope and healing after an abortion decision is achievable.

What is Abortion?

Abortion is the expulsion of a fetus from the uterus before it has reached the stage of viability, usually about the 20th week of gestation. An abortion can occur spontaneously, known as a miscarriage, or it may be induced purposefully.

Spontaneous abortions, or miscarriages, occur for various reasons, including disease, trauma, genetic defects, or biochemical incompatibility between mother and fetus. Occasionally, a fetus dies in the uterus but fails to be expelled, termed a missed abortion.

Induced abortions end a pregnancy with medication or a medical procedure. According to the American College of

Obstetricians and Gynecologists (ACOG), about one in four women in the U.S. will have an abortion by age 45. Banning or limiting abortion does not decrease the number of abortions performed but decreases the number of safe abortions, explains Dr. Jennifer Doorey, M.D., M.S.

The Christian View on Abortion

The Christian view on abortion is based on faith in Almighty God and His creating power in both natural and spiritual realms. The Bible, as the Word of God, guides how we conduct our lives. Our trust is in God, the Almighty Creator, who knows all things, including the lives of the unborn. We are called to live before Him in reverence and awe, with unwavering faith in His love, goodness, and wisdom. Any decision made with God brings rest and peace. Many lives could have been spared if God had been sought before these decisions were made.

Abortion Healing, Restoration, and Recovery

Having an abortion and regretting it later is a common experience. While what has been done cannot be undone, healing, restoration, and recovery are possible. The God of all comfort and healing can ease the sorrow and pain of an abortion, restoring life and joy.

Romans 3:22 offers good news for anyone who has had an abortion: "We are made right in God's sight when we trust in Jesus Christ to take away our sins. And we all can be saved in this same way, no matter who we are or what we have done." God offers forgiveness to anyone who asks for it, bringing peace of mind and heart. Abortion recovery begins with accepting that forgiveness, putting faith in Jesus, and allowing Him to have authority in your life.

How to Counsel a Woman Going Through Post-Abortion Stress

Post-Abortion Stress (PAS) is a traumatic stress disorder that many experience after an abortion. Counseling a woman going through PAS requires sensitivity and empathy. Here are some guidelines:

1. Provide a Safe and Non-Judgmental Space: Listen attentively and validate her emotions.

2. Acknowledge Unique Experiences: Recognize that every woman's experience with abortion is unique.

3. Help Explore Emotions: Encourage her to express her feelings related to the abortion.

4. Provide Information and Resources: Offer resources for medical and mental health support.

5. Encourage Self-Care: Suggest healthy practices such as sleep, exercise, and stress reduction.

6. Address Guilt and Shame: Help her work through these emotions non-judgmentally.

7. Connect with Support Groups: Recommend groups where she can connect with others with similar experiences.

8. Emphasize Healing: Reinforce that healing is possible and she can overcome her challenges.

Understanding Abortion and PAS

Abortion is a significant subject with profound implications. Biblical evidence suggests that an unborn baby is:

1. Completely Formed: The entire genetic makeup is present at conception.

2. Separate: The unborn baby is a separate person from the mother.

3. Unique: Each baby's chromosomes are unique.

4. Irreplaceable: Once a baby's life ends by abortion, that child can never be replaced.

America needs to change its mindset on this issue. 2 Chronicles 7:14 states, "If my people, who are called by my name, will humble themselves and pray and seek my face and turn from their wicked ways, then I will hear from heaven and will forgive their sin and will heal their land."

A woman suffering from PAS may struggle to process her emotions or grieve her loss. She needs to be at peace with God and those involved in her abortion decision and accept her God-given worth.

Stages of Post-Abortion Stress (PAS)

Women may experience stages of PAS differently. Here are common stages identified by experts:

a) Anger: Intense anger and resentment.

b) Grief: Deep loss and sadness.

c) Relief: Feeling relieved the crisis is over.

d) Rationalization: Logical explanations for the abortion.

Not all women experience all stages, and the duration and intensity may vary. Seeking support from family, friends, or a trained counselor can help navigate these stages.

Defense Mechanisms in PAS

Defense mechanisms shield individuals from painful memories, delaying freedom. Here are some mechanisms used by women suffering from PAS:

a) Denial: Refusing to accept reality.

b) Avoidance: Dismissing unacceptable truths.

c) Compensation: Exaggerating a strength to make up for a defect.

d) Reaction: Expressing the opposite of their true feelings.

Symptoms and Impact of PAS

PAS can have significant effects, such as:

1. Mental Health Issues: Depression, anxiety, PTSD.

2. Relationship Problems: Struggles with trust and intimacy.

3. Substance Abuse: Using drugs or alcohol to cope.

4. Guilt and Shame: Impacting self-esteem and sense of purpose.

5. Spiritual Struggles: Raising questions about faith.

Assisting Those with PAS

Support groups, counseling, and spiritual guidance provide safe spaces for healing. Here are some steps to assist those with PAS:

1. Encourage Turning to God: Psalm 34:18, "The Lord is near to the brokenhearted."

2. Remind of Forgiveness: 1 John 1:9, "If we confess our sins, He is faithful and just to forgive."

3. Encourage Self-Forgiveness: Matthew 6:14, "Forgive others and yourself."

4. Offer Practical Tools: Recommend support groups, self-care practices, and resources.

5. Seek Reconciliation: Romans 12:18, "Live peaceably with all."

Stages and Measures for Transformation

The 7 A's statements can assist in the road to transformation:

a) Admit: Admit personal responsibility (Hebrews 4:13).

b) Awaken: Awaken painful memories (Proverbs 20:5).

c) Acknowledge: Acknowledge anger (Ephesians 4:26-27).

d) Address: Address issues of guilt and shame (Psalm 32:5).

e) Agree: Agree to forgive (Colossians 3:13).

f) Acknowledge: Acknowledge grief (Ecclesiastes 3:4).

g) Acquire: Acquire a ministry of sharing hope (2 Corinthians 1:3-4).

Healing Measures for PAS

1. Admit Responsibility: Stop blaming others and agree that abortion was wrong.

2. Awaken Memories: Encourage positive self-attitude and avoid stress.

3. Acknowledge Anger: Express anger healthily without sinning (Ephesians 4:26-27).

4. Address Guilt/Shame: Stop self-condemnation and abusive behaviors.

5. Agree to Forgive: Choose to forgive as an act of will, not feeling.

6. Acknowledge Grief: Write feelings for the child, recognize the loss, and commit the child to God.

7. Acquire Sharing Hope: Express concern for others and lead them to Christ.

What Happens to the Baby After Abortion?

When someone asks what happens to their baby after an abortion, a Biblical counselor may refer to 2 Samuel 12:23. King David said about his deceased son, "I shall go to him, but he will not return to me." This suggests that the baby is with God in heaven, offering reassurance that the baby is in a place of love and peace.

God's forgiveness is available to all who seek it. Romans 8:1 assures no condemnation for those in Christ Jesus, and 1 John 1:9 promises forgiveness when we confess our sins. Healing and restoration after an abortion are possible through God's love and grace.

CHAPTER 3

Adultery: The Snare of an Affair

"Marriage should be honored by all, and the marriage bed kept pure, for God will judge the adulterer and all the sexually immoral." (Hebrews 13:4 NIV)

An affair refers to a romantic or sexual relationship between two people, typically one or both of whom are already in a committed relationship. Affairs can be incredibly destructive to all parties involved, as they often involve deceit, betrayal, and the breaking of trust.

The snare of an affair is that it can start out as something seemingly innocent but quickly escalate into something much more serious. It often begins with emotional intimacy or flirting, which can lead to physical intimacy and a full-blown affair.

The consequences of an affair can be devastating. It can lead to the breakup of marriages or relationships, emotional trauma, and a loss of trust and respect from others. Those involved often experience feelings of guilt, shame, and regret.

From a Biblical perspective, affairs are seen as a violation of the sanctity of marriage and a breaking of the commitment made between partners. The Bible teaches that marriage is a covenant between two people and God, and that it should be honored and respected.

To avoid the snare of an affair, it is important to prioritize one's marriage or committed relationship and to maintain open and honest communication with one's partner. Being aware of the warning signs of an affair, such as emotional distance, secrecy, and changes in behavior, is also crucial.

If a person finds themselves in the midst of an affair, it is important to seek guidance and support from a trusted counselor or religious leader. Repentance, confession, and seeking forgiveness from one's partner and from God can be important steps towards healing and restoration.

What is Adultery?

Adultery refers to the act of a married person engaging in a sexual relationship with someone who is not their spouse. It is a violation of the marriage covenant and a breaking of the commitment made between partners.

Adultery is often seen as a serious sin in many religious traditions, including Christianity. The Bible teaches that marriage is a covenant between a man and a woman, and that it should be honored and respected. The seventh commandment, "You shall not commit adultery" (Exodus 20:14), reinforces the importance of fidelity in marriage.

The consequences of adultery can be devastating. It can lead to the breakup of marriages and families, emotional trauma, and a loss of trust and respect from others. Those involved often experience feelings of guilt, shame, and regret.

From a Biblical perspective, adultery is seen as a sin that can have serious spiritual consequences. However, it is also seen as a sin that can be forgiven through repentance and seeking forgiveness from God and one's partner.

To avoid committing adultery, it is important to prioritize one's marriage and to maintain open and honest communication with one's spouse. Avoiding situations or relationships that could lead to temptation and seeking support and guidance from trusted friends or religious leaders can also help.

Why are People Drawn into Adultery?

Adultery is one of the most frequently and severely condemned sins in the Bible, mentioned 52 times. Reasons people are drawn into adultery include:

- Focusing on perceived needs.
- Rationalizing that God understands their situation.
- Blaming their marriage partner for their problems.
- Failing to consider lifelong consequences.
- Assuming their mate will never change.
- Believing it will make them happy.
- Opening the door of compromise.
- Thinking they won't get caught.
- Hardening their heart.
- Being lured by lust.

In the Old Testament, adultery was understood as sexual relations between a married (or betrothed) woman and a man other than her husband. It was considered a sin against the husband. Jesus extended this definition to include sexual relations between a married man and a woman other than his wife (Mark 10:11-12, Luke 16:18). Other New Testament teachings also understand it that way (1 Corinthians 6:15-16, 1 Corinthians 7:2).

The faithful spouse often knows when the partner has strayed, even without observing these outward signs. This intuition is believed to come from God, indicating that the bond between the two has been broken.

What are the Typical Signs of Infidelity?

The signs of infidelity or an affair can vary from person to person. Some common signs include:

1. Emotional distance: Your partner becomes emotionally distant.

2. Secretive behavior: Your partner hides their phone or computer.

3. Changes in routine: Your partner starts working late or going out more often without you.

4. Unusual spending: Your partner spends money in unusual ways, such as on gifts or hotel rooms.

5. Lack of intimacy: Your partner loses interest in physical intimacy.

6. Guilt or defensiveness: Your partner becomes defensive or guilty when asked questions.

7. Unexplained marks or smells: Your partner has unexplained marks on their body or smells of unfamiliar perfume or cologne.

Approach any suspicions of infidelity with sensitivity and communicate openly with your partner. Seeking guidance and support from a trusted counselor or religious leader can also be helpful.

Wise Biblical Counsel for Perpetrating Adultery

A Biblical counselor might advise the person committing adultery to stop for several reasons:

- The Bible forbids it.

- Your mate is wounded.

- Your peace is forfeited.

- Your health is jeopardized.

- Your future will not be blessed.

- Your morality is compromised.

- Your children lose their hero.

- Your conscience is scarred.

- Your integrity is destroyed.

- Your God condemns it.

Even though God will forgive adultery, the damage it causes often cannot be undone. It is extremely hurtful to the spouse and often leads to divorce, leaving the marriage partners embittered, disillusioned, and financially poorer. It robs children of love and security and denies them a good role model for their future marriages.

Showing True Change and Commitment

If a person committing adultery wants to show they have truly changed, they can:

1. Confess the adultery and seek forgiveness from God and their spouse.

2. Take responsibility: Acknowledge the impact of their actions and make amends.

3. Be transparent: Communicate openly about their whereabouts and interactions.

4. Seek counseling: Understand the root causes of their behavior and develop strategies to prevent future infidelity.

5. Be patient: Rebuilding trust takes time and patience.

6. Make changes: Avoid situations that could lead to temptation and prioritize their partner's needs.

7. Stay committed: Demonstrate love and commitment in both words and deeds.

Guiding the Faithful Mate

A Biblical counselor might guide the faithful mate with these do's and don'ts:

- Do use "I" statements to express feelings. (Matthew 18:15)

- Do express anger in non-destructive ways. (Ephesians 4:26)

- Do pray for guidance about possibly leaving an adulterous spouse. (Matthew 19:9)

- Do rely on the Lord for healing. (Jeremiah 17:14)

- Do choose to forgive. (Colossians 3:13)

- Don't try to please your mate excessively. (Exodus 14:14)

- Don't bring up specifics to change your mate. (John 16:8)

- Don't blame yourself for the adultery. (Romans 14:12)

- Don't minimize or deny the seriousness of the situation. (1 Corinthians 6:18)

- Don't seek to meet all your mate's needs. (Philippians 4:19)

- Don't believe you can't make it alone. (Psalm 62:5-6)

Why Adultery is Deceptive

Adultery gives the illusion of being loved, a flawed feeling of connection, and a false sense of security. These feelings are addictive, and when a marriage ends in divorce, the adulterous partner often brings that behavior into the next marriage, always seeking the emotional high that came the first time they committed adultery.

Conclusion

Adultery is a serious issue with significant consequences for all involved. By adhering to Biblical principles and seeking guidance from trusted counselors or religious leaders, individuals can work towards healing and restoration. Recognizing the deceptive nature of adultery and taking proactive steps to protect and prioritize one's marriage are crucial in maintaining a healthy and faithful relationship.

CHAPTER 4

Alcohol and Drug Abuse: Breaking Free and Staying Free

"A man is a slave to whatever has mastered him." (2 Peter 2:19)

Breaking Free and Staying Free from Alcohol and Drug Abuse

Alcohol and drug abuse are serious issues that can significantly impact a person's health, relationships, and overall quality of life. Breaking free from addiction can be a difficult journey, but with the right support and strategies, it is possible to achieve lasting recovery. Here are some tips for breaking free from alcohol and drug abuse and staying free:

1. Seek Help: Breaking free from addiction often requires professional help. Consider reaching out to a counselor, therapist, or addiction specialist who can help you develop a personalized treatment plan.

2. Build a Support Network: Surround yourself with people who support your recovery and can hold you accountable. This may include family members, friends, support groups, or a sponsor.

3. Develop Healthy Coping Strategies: Addiction often develops as a way to cope with stress, anxiety, or other difficult emotions. Developing healthy coping strategies, such as exercise, meditation, or creative pursuits, can help you manage these emotions in a healthy way.

4. Set Boundaries: Setting boundaries with people, places, or situations that trigger your addiction can help you stay on track with your recovery.

5. Practice Self-Care: Taking care of yourself is an important part of recovery. This may include getting enough sleep, eating a healthy diet, and practicing self-compassion.

6. Stay Motivated: Recovery is a journey, and it's important to stay motivated and focused on your goals. Consider setting small, achievable goals for yourself and celebrating your progress along the way.

Breaking free from addiction is a challenging process, but with the right support and strategies, it is possible to achieve lasting recovery and live a fulfilling life.

Drugs and Their Classifications

Drugs are generally classified into four major groups depending on their effect on the body. Excessive usage in any group can cause death. Proverbs 14:12 says, "There is a way that seems right to man, but in the end, it leads to death."

Drug Addiction

Drug addiction is a chronic, often relapsing brain disease that causes compulsive drug seeking and use, despite harmful consequences to the drug addict and those around them. Drugs control every waking moment of the addict's life, whether he or she is hooked on illegal street drugs, controlled substances, or lawful prescriptions. The individual's physical and psychological addiction is real and painful. For spouses of drug addicts, the pain is of a different sort, violating their finances, integrity, time, and emotional security. They may feel helpless to stop the addicted spouse from destroying everything that matters to them. However, drug addiction does not fall within specific biblical guidelines for divorce, so what can a spouse do?

Many situations are not directly addressed in Scripture, so we have to find applicable biblical principles. For example, cell phones and the Internet were unheard of when the Bible was completed, yet we can find principles that govern their use (see Psalm 101:3 and Matthew 6:33). The Bible does address drug use, always closely connected with sorcery and witchcraft.

The Greek word pharmakeia appears in Galatians 5:20 and Revelation 18:23, meaning "sorcery," specifically "the use of drugs and medicines related to spells." The word pharmakeia is the origin of the English words pharmacy, pharmacist, and pharmaceutical. Pharmaceuticals are related to witchcraft in that magicians and witches concocted potions used in casting spells or curses. The mind-altering chemicals put the user under the magician's control. Any connection with pharmakeia was harshly condemned in the Bible. In Galatians 5:20, drug addiction is listed along with idolatry and hatred as sins that control people and keep them from the kingdom of God.

Four Major Drug Classifications

1. Hallucinogens: Alter and distort reality, such as LSD, PCP, Marijuana, and Mescaline. They cause hallucinations, sensations, and images that seem completely real even though they are not.

2. Stimulants: Excite bodily functions and speed up the nervous system, such as cocaine, meth, crack, and amphetamines. They induce a powerful feeling of euphoria, a sense of well-being, suppressed appetite, and increased energy, but can result in hyperthermia, cardiovascular abnormalities, and sudden death.

3. Narcotics: Reduce pain and elevate a person's mood, such as morphine, opium, codeine, heroin, methadone, and meperidine.

4. Depressants: Produce a calming effect and slow down the nervous system, such as alcohol, sedatives, barbiturates, tranquilizers, and organic solvents. They cause symptoms like poor concentration, lack of judgment, and slurred speech, and can lead to tolerance, requiring larger doses to achieve the initial effects.

Psychological and Physical Effects

1. Hallucinogens: Physical effects vary, including eyes fixed in a blank stare or moving rapidly, slurred or blocked speech, with a higher rate of accidents and violence.

2. Stimulants: Symptoms include excitability, increased energy, heightened self-confidence, hyperactivity, dilated pupils, rapid, unclear speech, and high blood pressure.

3. Narcotics: Symptoms include dulled senses, confusion, temporary euphoria, droopy eyelids, relief of pain, constricted pupils, and slowed reaction and motor skills.

4. Depressants: Symptoms include poor concentration, lack of judgment, aggressiveness, decreased pulse, BP, respiration, energy, and slurred speech.

Biblical Perspective on Intoxication and Addiction

Isaiah 28:7 refers to those who are intoxicated with depressants as those who stagger from wine and reel from beer, suggesting that drunkenness leads to error and takes us away from wisdom and God's will. Even the priest and the prophet in this Scripture reference found themselves under the tyranny of drunkenness.

Stimulants excite bodily functions and speed up the central nervous system, often resulting in exaggerated self-confidence and emotional instability. Proverbs 6:15 says, "Disaster will overtake him in an instant and he will suddenly be destroyed, without remedy." Although the Bible doesn't directly mention hallucinogens, it addresses the disturbing hallucinogenic effects of alcohol.

Psalm 69:29 encourages us to seek the Lord for direction instead of drugs for pain relief, to depend on Him: "I am in pain and distress, may your salvation, O God, protect me."

The Impact of Intoxication

Intoxication causes changes in behavior, including mood changes, faulty judgment, slurred speech, poor coordination, unsteady gait, and impaired social functioning. The abuse of wine began early in the Bible with Noah getting drunk and being seen in a shameful state (Genesis 9:20-27) and Lot's daughters getting him drunk to sin (Genesis 19:30-38). Over and over, the Bible shows alcohol as causing one to set aside good judgment (Proverbs 20:1; 23:29-35; 31:2-9; Isaiah 5:21-23; 56:9-12; Hosea 4:11-12).

To be drunk is to live without self-control, a fruit of the Spirit (Galatians 5:16-21, 23; 2 Timothy 1:7), living under the control of wine and evil impulses and desires. Intoxication may result in coma or death and is described in Dorland's Illustrated Medical Dictionary as a state of being poisoned. Deuteronomy 32:32-33

Abuse and Addiction

Abuse occurs when the use of drugs results in a person's failure to fulfill responsibilities or maintain healthy relationships or when putting the individual or others at harm. In 1 Corinthians 11:17-34, some Corinthians over-indulged in food and drink (see verse 21), leading to a shameful celebration of the Lord's death and even judgment.

Addiction occurs when a person experiences these indicators:

1. Drug Tolerance: Needing increasingly more to obtain the same effect.

2. Physical Dependence: Suffering from withdrawal symptoms like nausea, sweating, shaking, and anxiety.

3. Craving: Developing a pattern of compulsive drug use.

Withdrawal occurs when the distress caused by a lack of the drug severely disrupts a person's daily life (Isaiah 24:9,11).

Addressing Drug Dependence

A wise Biblical counselor might advise a person who asks, "How can I be held responsible for my drug dependence when most drugs are addictive and cause the addiction?" (1 Samuel 1:14)

Your drug dependence has been created both by your choice to use drugs and the drugs themselves. Intoxication results from the makeup of the drug you use and the way it is metabolized by your body. The only way to avoid addiction is to make deliberate choices to stop abusing drugs. 1 Samuel 1:14 says: "How long will you keep on getting drunk? Get rid of your wine."

Alcohol and drugs take control of our bodies and our lives. We are to live under the control of God's Spirit, to His glory. Drunkenness and drug use thus have no place in the life of the Christian.

Anger: Facing the Fire Within

"An angry man stirs up dissension, and a hot-tempered one commits many sins." (Proverbs 29:22)

What is Anger?

Anger is a normal and natural emotion that we all experience from time to time. It is often described as a feeling of intense displeasure or irritation, usually in response to a perceived threat or injustice. Anger can range in intensity from mild frustration to intense rage and can be expressed in various ways, from passive aggression to explosive outbursts.

Anger is a complex emotion that can have both positive and negative effects. On the positive side, anger can help us protect ourselves and stand up for our rights. It can also motivate us to make positive changes in our lives or in the world around us. On the negative side, anger can be destructive if not managed properly. Uncontrolled anger can damage relationships, harm our physical and mental health, and lead to aggressive or violent behavior.

It's important to note that while anger is a natural emotion, it's not always justified. Sometimes our anger is based on misunderstandings, unrealistic expectations, or past traumas. Learning to recognize and manage our anger in a healthy way can help us respond more effectively to the challenges we face and improve our overall well-being.

Facing the Fire Within and Breaking from Anger

The Four Degrees of Anger and Their Meaning:

1. Fury: A fiery anger so fierce that it destroys common sense.

2. Indignation: A simmering anger provoked by something unjust, often perceived as justified.

3. Rage: A blazing anger resulting in a loss of self-control, often to the extreme of violence and temporary insanity.

4. Wrath: A burning anger accompanied by a desire to avenge.

Sometimes, anger can get out of control and turn destructive. Unlike anger, rage involves a scenario where a person is not handling their anger properly. While anger itself does not necessarily lead to violence, rage can lead to physical aggression.

A person's initial response to a feeling of anger is a God-given emotion. If you express your anger but do not let the sun go down on it, it is not sin (Ephesians 4:26). Anger signals that something is wrong and propels a person into action, causing them to stop, evaluate, and take appropriate action.

Everyone gets angry from time to time. Anger can be understood as a gift from God that allows us to recognize and respond to wrongs or injustices. People who deal effectively with anger respond properly to the daily challenges around us. As Paul put it in Romans 8:37, we know that with Christ we can be "more than conquerors."

All anger has a source, often derived from a loss or threat to our God-given inner needs for unconditional love, security, and significance, or conflicts with our inner moral code that produces a sense of right or wrong within us.

Sources of Anger

1. Fear: Anger occurs when a person's future feels threatened, possibly due to a threat of loss to their security brought on by a change in circumstances.

2. Injustice: Anger occurs when a person senses a perceived violation of their inner moral code or feels that they, or a loved one, have been wronged or treated unfairly.

3. Hurt: Anger occurs because of a wounded heart from rejection or emotional pain. This type of anger can become a protective wall to keep people and pain away.

4. Frustration: Anger occurs when a person's efforts are thwarted or unsuccessful, and their sense of significance is threatened.

If a person feels their rights have been violated from a real or perceived injustice and holds on to that offense without dealing with it, it will find a home in their heart. This person may live with an attitude of offense for the rest of their lives.

Simply observing the life and death of Jesus teaches us about dealing with anger, injustice, and conflict in loving ways. Note how, when Jesus was being crucified, He said, "Father, forgive them, for they do not know what they are doing."

Be the first to say "I'm sorry" or to offer empathy and compassion. This is not always fair, but do it anyway because God does it for you. You can "Forgive as the Lord forgave you" (Colossians 3:13).

Frustration from unmet expectations, whether personal or from others, is a major source of anger. Unresolved anger can rob a person's heart of peace and contentment and hinder their relationship with God and others.

Healing and Resolution of Unresolved Anger
Acknowledge Your Anger:

1. Admit you are angry.

2. Be aware of when you feel angry.

3. Avoid suppressing or repressing your anger out of fear.

4. Take responsibility for any inappropriate anger (Proverbs 28:13).

Another good way to sort out your feelings with God is to "take a break." Give yourself a time-out to think things through before they escalate.

Analyze Your Style:

1. How often do you feel angry?

2. How do you know when you are angry?

3. How do others know when you are angry?

4. How do you release your anger? (Psalm 139:23-24).

Assess the Source:

1. Seek help to understand the source of your anger (hurt, injustice, fear, frustration) (Psalm 51:6).

Before reacting, pray and reflect on the problem and practical solutions. Righteous anger aims to solve problems, not exacerbate them.

Appraise Your Thinking:

1. Are you expecting others to meet your standards?

2. Are you guilty of distorted thinking?

3. Are you exaggerating the situation?

4. Are you assuming the worst?

5. Are you labeling one action based on other actions?

6. Are you generalizing with statements like "You never..." or "You always...?" (Proverbs 21:29).

Admit Your Needs:

1. Do you use anger to manipulate and demand love?

2. Do you use explosive anger to feel significant?

3. Do you use controlling anger to feel secure?

4. Do you know that only Christ can meet all your needs? (Philippians 4:19).

Angry people often live in a love-starved state. Responding with pure love can fulfill their real craving. "Love your enemies, bless those who curse you, do good to those who hate you, and pray for those who persecute you" (Matthew 5:44-45).

Abandon Your Demands:

1. Instead of demanding that others meet your needs, look to the Lord to meet them (Jeremiah 31:3).

2. 2 Peter 1:3 says, 'By his divine power, God has given us everything we need for living a godly life.' (Jeremiah 29:11, Psalm 118:6).

Alter Your Attitudes:

1. Have the goal to be like-minded with Christ.

2. Do not think of yourself first.

3. Give the other person preferential treatment.

4. Consider the other person's interest.

5. Have the attitude of Jesus Christ.

6. Do not emphasize your position or rights.

7. Look for ways to demonstrate a servant's heart.

8. Speak and act with a humble spirit (Philippians 2:2-8).

Developing humility is an antidote to toxic anger. Humility is the opposite of arrogance, entitlement, superiority, and contempt. These attitudes incite anger, whereas humility fosters peace. "For everyone who exalts himself will be humbled, and he who humbles himself will be exalted" (Luke 14:11).

Address Your Anger:

1. Determine whether your anger is justified.

2. Decide on the appropriate response.

3. Depend on the Holy Spirit for guidance.

4. Develop constructive dialogue when confronting.

5. Avoid speaking from a heart of unforgiveness.

We live in an anger-infested world. Seek to bring peace into situations. Don't stoke the flames of fiery arguments. Put biblical principles for getting along above personal opinions and arguments.

1. Don't use phrases like "How could you…?" or "Why can't you…?" Use personal statements, like "I feel…"

2. Don't bring up past grievances. Stay focused on the present issue.

3. Don't assume the other person is wrong. Listen for feedback.

4. Don't expect instant understanding. Be patient and respond with gentleness.

5. Demonstrate the grace of God by saying phrases like "I am crucified with Christ" (Galatians 2:20).

If we learn to deal with anger as Jesus taught, we will live more in God's peace. The way of Christ helps us to forgive, find security and strength in God's love, bless others (even difficult ones), and resolve relationship conflicts.

CHAPTER 6

Anorexia and Bulimia: Control That Is Out of Control

"And I pray that you, being rooted and established in love, may have power, together with all the Lord's holy people, to grasp how wide and long and high and deep is the love of Christ, and to know this love that surpasses knowledge—that you may be filled to the measure of all the fullness of God." (Ephesians 3:16-19)

What Are Anorexia and Bulimia?

Anorexia and bulimia are two types of eating disorders characterized by unhealthy patterns of food intake and weight control. Anorexia involves an intense fear of gaining weight, a distorted body image, and severe restriction of food intake, often leading to dangerously low body weight. Bulimia involves cycles of binge eating followed by purging behaviors, such as vomiting, using laxatives or diuretics, or excessive exercise.

Both disorders can have serious physical and emotional consequences. They can lead to malnutrition, electrolyte imbalances, gastrointestinal problems, and other health issues. Emotionally, they can cause depression, anxiety, and social isolation.

Treatment for anorexia and bulimia typically involves a combination of medical care, nutritional counseling, and therapy. The primary goal is to restore physical health and address the underlying emotional and psychological factors that contribute to the eating disorder. This may involve cognitive-behavioral therapy, family therapy, or other forms of psychotherapy.

If you or someone you know is struggling with anorexia or bulimia, it's important to seek professional help. Early intervention can improve the chances of successful recovery and reduce the risk of long-term physical and emotional consequences. Individuals suffering from anorexia and bulimia are often starving for unconditional love and acceptance.

Bulimia: The Psychological Eating Disorder

Bulimia is a psychological eating disorder characterized by repeated binge-and-purge episodes. Food is often eaten to meet emotional needs, resulting in guilt and fear of gaining weight, which prompts self-induced vomiting. The food is usually eaten secretly and gobbled down rapidly with little chewing, ending a binge by abdominal discomfort. When the binge is over, the person feels guilty and purges to rid the body of excess calories. Excessive concern with shape and weight is characteristic of those with bulimia.

Anorexia: The Self-Starvation Disorder

Anorexia is a psychological eating disorder characterized by chronic self-starvation, rooted in a distorted body image and an abnormal fear of gaining weight. Anorexics often feel they don't deserve to live and have made too many mistakes. In acute stages, an anorexic may try to harm themselves and become so exhausted from mental battles that they see no hope in continuing to seek help.

Problems Associated with Eating Disorders

Common issues include:

1. Deception: Stealing food, using laxatives, pretending to swallow food, or lying about eating.

2. Compulsion: Controlling some area of their life, thinking, "Eating is the one part of my life I can control."

3. People-pleasing: Thoughts like, "If I had just done better or looked better, they would love me."

4. Perfectionism: Thoughts like, "I must perform perfectly. I must look like magazine models."

5. Loneliness: Feeling alone and unable to talk to anyone about their problem.

6. Depression: Logical thinking becomes virtually impossible; life becomes a deliberate attempt at suicide.

7. Confusion: Valuing achievement versus appearance, intelligence versus thinness.

8. Low self-worth: Having thoughts like, "I'm a fat pig. I don't deserve to live."

Physical Consequences of Eating Disorders

Match the warning signs and possible abnormalities associated with anorexia or bulimia:

1. Digestive Problems: Forced vomiting causing a bleeding esophagus, bloated stomach, stomach cramps, and chronic constipation.

2. Kidney Failure: Chronic dehydration causing kidneys to fail.

3. Weight Swings or Drops: Binging and purging cause extreme weight fluctuations; self-starvation causes dangerously low body weight.

4. Dental Problems: Purging brings up hydrochloric acid that erodes tooth enamel.

5. Hypoglycemia: Low blood sugar causing headaches, dizziness, fatigue, and anxiety.

6. Vision Problems: Deficiency of Vitamin A causing eyesight deterioration.

7. Bowel Dysfunction: Excessive laxative use causing bowels to become dependent.

8. Heart Problems: Malnutrition causing an imbalance of heart's essential minerals.

9. Musculoskeletal Problems: Deficiency in potassium causing muscle spasms and pain.

10. Bone Problems: Deficiency in calcium causing bone deterioration and fractures.

11. Hair Loss: Poor nutrition causing thinning hair and balding.

12. Menstrual Problems: Deficiency in fat causing menstrual cycles to stop.

13. Mental Difficulties: Malnutrition causes slow thinking and extreme forgetfulness.

14. Blood Cell Abnormalities: Anemia and low white blood counts cause immune system deficiencies.

15. Glandular Problems: Thyroid irregularities causing decreased energy and lethargy.

Psychological and Social Issues

People with eating disorders often struggle with feelings of inadequacy, hopelessness, powerlessness, and worthlessness. They may have experienced abuse or lived in high-performance atmospheres. Both anorexics and bulimics have an obsessive focus on being thin but also love food. They may believe they can only acquire love if they are thin.

Counseling and Recovery

A counselor might say, "The issue in life is not my size, but to see myself through God's eyes. The Lord loves me just as I am. Instead of being consumed by control, I am choosing to release control of my life and trust the Lord Jesus with every part of my heart" (Proverbs 3:5-6).

Steps to Recovery

1. Agree to get a thorough medical checkup: This condition is life-threatening (Proverbs 27:12).

2. Attend regular counseling sessions: Seek help from a knowledgeable professional (Proverbs 23:12).

3. Acquire knowledge about eating disorders: Educate yourself and those close to you (Proverbs 24:14).

4. Admit your inability to control the eating problem: Confess your struggles (James 5:16).

5. Abandon the idea that you just need more willpower: Understand that this is not a diet problem (2 Corinthians 10:4-5; 2 Corinthians 12:9-10).

6. Allow yourself to forgive those who have hurt you and yourself: Embrace forgiveness (Colossians 3:13).

7. Act in total faith on God's power to rescue you: Trust in God's deliverance (Psalm 71:1-3).

8. Accept your true worth: Know that you are worth Jesus' dying for you—you are dearly loved (John 3:16, 2 Corinthians 5:17).

Supporting Someone in Recovery

When a person suffering from anorexia or bulimia relapses, a wise counselor can assist them by providing support through:

1. Learning everything you can: Knowledge is your friend (Proverbs 19:20).

2. Confronting in a loving way: Confrontation can be an act of love (Proverbs 12:18).

3. Encouraging professional help: Seeking help is a mark of wisdom (Proverbs 15:22).

4. Talking about emotions: Reach deeper levels of communication (Proverbs 20:5).

5. Listening with your heart: Listening builds trust and opens communication (Ecclesiastes 3:7).

6. Valuing genuine love: Use compassionate terms to nurture (Proverbs 25:11).

7. Expressing love with appropriate physical affection: Eye contact and touch can convey care (Proverbs 17:17).

8. Being honest about the dangers: Highlight the long-term dangers (1 Thessalonians 5:14).

Don'ts in Counseling

1. Don't be forceful or controlling: Distract from negative thoughts with praise and love (Proverbs 12:18).

2. Don't be unrealistic about expectations: Healing can take time (Proverbs 19:11).

3. Don't let anorexics see their weight when being weighed: Avoid giving them a negative number to fight (Proverbs 16:21).

4. Don't fail to request help from a former anorexic: They know the tricks and can provide support (Proverbs 27:17).

5. Don't assume you are helpless if anorexics won't eat: Offer to hand-feed to relieve their pressure (Galatians 6:2).

6. Don't give up: Patience, persistence, and perseverance are essential (1 Corinthians 13:4, 7-8).

Finding Love and Control in God

People with eating disorders often feel they have no control and focus on food. Eating disorders are contrary to God's plan for us. Binging, purging, and starving are not God's ways of treating the body. "Don't you know that your body is the temple of the Holy Spirit, who lives in you and was given to you by God? You do not belong to yourself, for God bought you with a high price. So, you must honor

God with your body" (1 Corinthians 6:19-20). True beauty and worth are found in one's identity in Christ, not in one's weight, appearance, or accomplishments.

CHAPTER 7

Childhood Sexual Abuse: The Secret Storm

"He lies in wait like a lion in cover; He lies in wait to catch the helpless; he catches the helpless and drags them off in his net." (Psalm 10:9)

Understanding Childhood Sexual Abuse

Childhood sexual abuse involves any form of sexual activity between an adult or older adolescent and a child under 18. This can include behaviors ranging from touching or fondling to penetration. The impact of such abuse is profound, leading to lasting physical, emotional, and psychological effects.

Survivors often struggle with shame, guilt, and self-blame. Symptoms of post-traumatic stress disorder (PTSD), such as flashbacks, nightmares, and anxiety, are common. Trust issues and difficulties in forming healthy relationships often persist into adulthood.

It's crucial for survivors to know they are not alone and that help is available. Therapy, support groups, and hotlines can provide the necessary support and tools for healing. Reporting abuse to authorities and seeking medical attention when needed are important steps in the recovery process.

If you suspect a child is being sexually abused, take immediate action to protect them. This includes reporting to authorities, offering support and resources to the child and family, and working to prevent further abuse. Childhood sexual abuse instills deep shame in victims, often too young to articulate their trauma, leading to a lifetime of PTSD, depression, and anxiety if untreated.

Incest: A Grave Violation

Incest involves sexual interaction with a child by a family member, whether by blood, adoption, or marriage. The Bible explicitly condemns incest: "No one is to approach any close relative to have sexual relations" (Leviticus 18:6).

Statistics reveal that children are three times more likely to be victims of rape than adults, with most abuse perpetrated by someone the child knows. This abuse is usually premeditated, following a pattern: seduction, stimulation, silence, and suppression, leaving the child feeling hopeless and powerless.

According to childtrauma.org, one in three females and one in five males in the U.S. have been sexually abused before turning 18. The American Academy of Experts in Traumatic Stress (AAETS) reports that 30% of male children and 40% of female children have been molested in some way.

Patterns of Abuse

Perpetrators follow a typical pattern of behavior:

1. Seduction: The perpetrator gains the child's trust through intimacy, gifts, or money, creating an emotional bond.

2. Stimulation: The child experiences physical touch that feels appropriate and warm, leading to desensitization and vulnerability to more advanced sexual activity.

3. Silence: The perpetrator ensures the child's silence through intimidation and threats, leveraging their power over the child.

4. Suppression: The child feels alone and powerless, leading to emotional enslavement and hopelessness.

It is crucial to recognize that the child's natural bodily response to sexual stimulation does not equate to consent or enjoyment. No guilt should ever be attributed to the child, only to the abuser.

The Impact of Abuse

Sexual abuse can lead to hyper-sexualization or sexual dysfunction and self-destructive behavior in later life. The child may eventually disclose the abuse, often feeling betrayed and hopeless when there is no one to rescue them.

After the abuse, perpetrators fear being discovered and often shift blame to the child, causing further emotional damage.

Addressing Child Sexual Abuse

Facing the truth that child abuse is occurring is the first step towards healing. Awareness and action are crucial.

Do's and Don'ts of Awareness:

1. Do report child abuse as it is a crime.

2. Do recognize that children are usually abused by someone they know.

3. Do understand that sexual abuse may not always be physically violent.

4. Do believe children who disclose abuse, even if they deny or change their stories out of fear.

5. Do intervene, as sexual abuse is progressive and will worsen if not stopped.

6. Don't deny the possibility of abuse.

7. Don't minimize the abuse or let the offender go without confrontation.

8. Don't keep abuse a family secret or blame other family members.

When child abuse is suspected, the first step for a Biblical counselor is to seek professional help trained to work with children. Verify or relieve your suspicions by contacting professionals, child advocacy programs, family attorneys, spiritual leaders, shelters, Child Protective Services, the police, or the district attorney's office.

Responding to Disclosures of Abuse

If a child discloses sexual abuse, respond with compassion and take the following steps:

1. Listen and believe the child: Provide a safe, supportive environment for them to share their story.

2. Reassure the child: Make sure they understand that the abuse was not their fault.

3. Report the abuse: Comply with mandatory reporting laws and organizational policies.

4. Provide support and resources: Help the child access medical care or counseling.

5. Maintain confidentiality: Share information only on a need-to-know basis.

Practical Steps and Follow-Up

1. Take the child for immediate medical examination and documentation.

2. Report the abuse to appropriate authorities and maintain a record of all contacts and actions taken.

3. Follow up with caseworkers regularly.

4. Provide continuous support and ensure the child receives professional counseling.

Opening Hearts and Breaking Secrecy

To help a child disclose abuse:

1. Pray for wisdom.

2. Provide a safe environment.

3. Ask gentle, non-leading questions.

4. Listen carefully and affirm the child's feelings.

5. Involve authorities with expertise in child abuse.

6. Communicate belief and support to the child.

Role-Playing for Assertiveness

Role-playing can help a child learn to say no to inappropriate advances and other bad actions. Using puppets or similar tools can make this process more engaging for young children.

The Perpetrator's Weapon: Secrecy

Secrecy is the most powerful weapon of a perpetrator, maintaining control and continuing the abuse without consequences. They use threats, manipulation, and coercion to keep the abuse hidden. Breaking this secrecy by reporting the abuse is crucial to protect the child and hold the perpetrator accountable.

God's Strategy: Love, Compassion, and Justice

God's strategy against child abuse is grounded in love, compassion, and justice. Children are precious in God's sight, and those who harm them face His wrath. As Biblical counselors, we must show love and compassion to abused children, speak out against injustice, and protect the vulnerable.

Children hold a special place in God's heart. Jesus welcomed children and blessed them, promoting their well-being and condemning any harm against them. The Bible calls for child blessing, not child abuse.

CHAPTER 8

Codependency: Balancing an Unbalanced Relationship

"A man is a slave to whatever has mastered him." (2 Peter 2:19)

Understanding Codependency

Codependency is a pattern of behavior in which someone excessively relies on their partner or another person to meet their emotional and psychological needs. Codependent individuals may prioritize their partner's needs and wants over their own, often at the expense of their well-being. This dynamic creates an unbalanced relationship characterized by manipulation and control, draining joy and happiness from life.

Identifying a Codependent Relationship

A person could be in a codependent relationship if they:

1. Feel a loss of personal identity

2. Violate their conscience

3. Have difficulty establishing healthy, intimate relationships

4. Struggle with low self-worth

5. Control and manipulate

6. Have difficulty setting boundaries

7. Become jealous and possessive

8. Fear abandonment

9. Experience extreme ups and downs

10. Have a false sense of security

11. Have another addiction besides the relationship

12. Feel trapped in the relationship

Biblical Counseling for Codependency

A biblical counselor can help someone struggling with codependency by:

1. Encouraging Self-Care: Emphasizing the importance of prioritizing their own needs and setting boundaries.

2. Identifying Unhealthy Patterns: Helping the individual recognize and address unhealthy dynamics in their relationships.

3. Seeking Support: Providing information about local support groups or resources that can aid in their healing and growth.

4. Developing a Relationship with God: Guiding them to find their worth and purpose in God, rather than in others.

Steps to Overcoming Codependency

Step 1: Confronting Codependency

1. Admit the Truth:

- To yourself: Examine if your life is consumed by thoughts of another person, if you take care of others to your detriment, or if you cover up for a loved one's addiction.

- To a trustworthy person: Confess to someone who can hold you accountable.

- To God: Seek divine guidance and strength.

2. Confront the Consequences:

- Accept responsibility for past actions and how they have hurt relationships and yourself.

- Acknowledge the pain caused by jealousy, envy, selfishness, or obsession.

- Recognize how codependency has weakened your relationship with God.

3. Confront Painful Emotions:

- Understand that pain is inevitable, whether you stay or leave the codependent relationship.

- Expect emotional withdrawal and seek support from others.

4. Confront the Relationship:

- Acknowledge your role and stop relating through codependent patterns.

- Replace destructive behaviors with constructive ones.

- Focus on God's purpose to conform you to Christ's character.

5. Confront Your Focus:

- Stop focusing on what the other person is doing and start focusing on becoming emotionally healthy.

- Solve your own problems rather than trying to change the other person.

6. Confront What You Need to Leave:

- Leave dependent thinking and immature needs.

- Nurture balanced relationships and seek emotional independence.

7. Build Mature Relationships:

- Establish interdependent, emotionally balanced relationships.

- Set personal boundaries and maintain them.

Step 2: Look at Past Love Addictions

1. Journaling: Reflect on past relationships to understand patterns and emotional stages.

Step 3: Pursuing Interdependent Relationships

1. Spiritual Growth:

- Engage in Bible study and group prayer.

- Read God's Word daily and memorize Scripture.

- Find an accountability group and a Christian mentor.

2. Reconnect with Friends and Family: Rebuild relationships that may have been neglected.

3. Personal Time: Engage in activities you enjoy.

4. Join a Church Group: Actively participate and contribute.

5. Seek Professional Help: Talk to a faith-based counselor to rebuild your sense of self.

6. Make a Plan:

- Ask God for discernment.

- Seek help from a mentor.

- Set appropriate goals with your accountability group.

7. Resolve Unhealthy Patterns with Parents: Address any lingering issues.

8. Create a New Job Description:

- Discern character and respond maturely.

- Be a safe person and be present in relationships.

- Establish clear boundaries.

Step 4: Effective Communication

1. Communicate Convictions:

- Express the need for change, forgiveness, and limits of responsibility.

- Release control and trust God.

2. Release Others:

- Love without leaning, care without controlling, and trust God's control.

- Accept that your help may have been harmful and embrace healing.

God's Answer: Interdependency

Christian interdependence, where both parties rely on each other for completion, is vital. This concept, found in Genesis 2:24 and 1 Peter 4:10, emphasizes mutual support and service rather than self-centeredness. Embrace interdependence in Christ, fostering love, selflessness, and the exercise of spiritual gifts for the benefit of others. This opposes the selfishness and destructiveness of codependency.

Crisis Intervention: Caring Enough to Confront

Crisis intervention is a critical skill for a biblical counselor, as it involves providing immediate assistance and support to individuals who are experiencing a crisis or a traumatic event. Here are some steps that a biblical counselor can take to provide effective crisis intervention:

1. Establish Rapport and Create a Safe Space:

It is essential to create a safe, non-judgmental space for the individual to share their experiences and feelings. The counselor should establish rapport with the individual by actively listening, showing empathy, and demonstrating a genuine concern for their well-being.

2. Assess the Situation:

The counselor should assess the situation to determine the severity of the crisis and the level of intervention required. This may involve asking questions to understand the individual's needs, identifying any potential risks, and ensuring the individual's physical and emotional safety.

3. Provide Emotional Support:

Crisis intervention involves providing emotional support and reassurance to the individual. The counselor can help the individual cope with their emotions by offering validation, encouragement, and comfort. This may include practical suggestions for self-care and stress reduction.

4. Offer Practical Assistance:

Depending on the nature of the crisis, the counselor may need to offer practical assistance to the individual. This could involve providing referrals to community resources, coordinating with other professionals, or helping the individual access emergency services.

5. Follow Up and Provide Ongoing Support:

Crisis intervention is not a one-time event but an ongoing process. The counselor should follow up with the individual to ensure they are receiving the support they need and provide ongoing care and guidance as needed.

By establishing rapport, assessing the situation, providing emotional support, offering practical assistance, and providing ongoing support, biblical counselors can help individuals navigate through crises and move toward healing and restoration.

Biblical Guidance for Crisis Intervention

Matthew 18:15-16:

"If your brother sins against you, go and show him his fault, just between the two of you. If he listens to you, you have won your brother over. But if he will not listen, take one or two others along, so that 'every matter may be established by the testimony of two or three witnesses.'"

It's essential to address issues directly with the person involved rather than gossiping or sharing with others under the guise of seeking counsel. Speak to the party directly, one-on-one.

Ezekiel 3:18-19:

"When I say to a wicked man, 'You will surely die,' and you do not warn him or speak out to dissuade him from his evil ways in order to save his life, that wicked man will die for his sin, and I will hold you accountable for his blood."

The goal of group crisis intervention is not just to set someone on the path to recovery but to guide them toward transformation and Christlike maturity.

Addressing Harmful Habits

Crisis intervention confrontations can address harmful habits, such as:

- Objects: Dependence on substances like alcohol, tobacco, cocaine, or sexual addiction to erotic items, pornographic materials, and sex toys.

- Behaviors: Inappropriate sexual activities, excessive spending, gambling, and addictions to love or a "savior" complex.

Steps to Helping Someone in Crisis

1. Pray for Wisdom and Understanding:

Seek guidance from the Lord (Psalm 32:8; Proverbs 2:6). The threefold repetition in Psalm 32:8 highlights the importance of not only pointing out faults but also guiding and teaching.

2. Educate Yourself:

Understand the specific addiction or sin and explore appropriate crisis intervention programs (Proverbs 18:15). Pray first for divine insight into the underlying issues.

3. Seek Professional Help:

Contact a counseling office for a referral to a Christian leader trained in crisis intervention procedures (Proverbs 15:22).

4. Plan the Approach:

Meet with an intervention specialist to discuss counseling options and the potential impact on the individual and their family (Proverbs 19:20).

5. Enlist Key People:

Involve caring family members, friends, and respected individuals affected by the person's behavior who are willing to confront them (Proverbs 14:25).

6. Confidential Initial Meeting:

Hold a meeting with key people without the individual present to plan the intervention.

7. Confront the Individual:

Hold a second meeting with the individual present. Each key person should express their concerns and care, using personalized statements (Proverbs 12:18). Speak graciously and with wisdom (Colossians 4:6).

Making Effective Intervention Statements: The Six P's of Appeal

1. The Personal
2. The Past
3. The Pain
4. The Plea
5. The Plan
6. The Price

Conducting the Intervention

- Start with Prayer: Pray individually, with the group, and if possible, with the person needing help.

- Stay Calm: Remain composed even when emotions rise.

- Manage Responses: Control your responses and set limits.

- Handle Challenges: Address challenging questions and prevent physical confrontations.

The 'Don'ts' of Dialogue

1. Don't call names, preach, or be judgmental.
2. Don't argue if facts are disputed.

3. Don't defend the offender when others make their statements.

4. Don't accept promises without commitment to immediate action.

5. Don't overreact; keep emotions under control.

6. Don't shield your loved one from consequences.

7. Don't give ultimatums unless prepared to follow through.

Outcome of Crisis Intervention

The individual will either seek help immediately or face the consequences of refusing treatment. The guiding purpose should be aligned with James 5:19-20, which emphasizes the importance of turning a sinner from their ways to save them from death and cover a multitude of sins.

By following these steps and biblical principles, counselors can effectively intervene in crises, offering guidance, support, and a path towards healing and transformation.

CHAPTER 10

Critical Spirit: Changing the Heart of a Critic

"You, then, why do you judge your brother? Or why do you look down on your brother? For we will all stand before God's judgment seat." (Romans 14:10)

A critical spirit is a negative attitude characterized by fault-finding, harsh criticism, and a judgmental outlook towards others. It is a destructive behavior that causes pain and hurt to those around us and hinders our own spiritual growth and well-being. As biblical counselors, it is important to address and help individuals overcome a critical spirit. Here are some steps that a biblical counselor can take to help an individual change their critical spirit:

1. Identify the Root Cause:

A critical spirit can stem from various underlying issues, such as low self-esteem, insecurity, fear, or unresolved past hurts. The counselor should work with the individual to identify the root cause of their critical spirit, as this will help develop a more effective approach to addressing the behavior. "Search me, God, and know my heart; test me and know my anxious thoughts" (Psalm 139:23).

2. Encourage Self-Reflection:

A critical spirit often stems from a lack of self-awareness and an inability to recognize the impact of our words and actions on others. The counselor should encourage the individual to engage in self-reflection and become more aware of their thoughts, feelings, and behaviors. "Examine yourselves to see whether you are in the faith; test yourselves" (2 Corinthians 13:5).

3. Foster a Culture of Grace:

Criticism and judgment can create a culture of fear and shame, making it difficult for individuals to change. The counselor should foster a culture of grace and acceptance, where individuals feel safe to share their struggles and receive support and encouragement. "Bear with each other and forgive one another if any of you has a grievance against someone. Forgive as the Lord forgave you" (Colossians 3:13).

4. Develop Empathy and Compassion:

A critical spirit often stems from a lack of empathy and compassion towards others. The counselor should work with the individual to develop empathy and compassion, helping them understand the perspective of others and recognize their own biases and prejudices. "Finally, all of you, be like-minded, be sympathetic, love one another, be compassionate and humble" (1 Peter 3:8).

5. Encourage Positive Communication:

The counselor should encourage the individual to communicate in a positive and constructive way, focusing on the strengths and positive qualities of others rather than their faults and weaknesses. This can help shift their mindset from a critical to a more constructive and positive perspective. "Do not let any unwholesome talk come out of your mouths, but only what is helpful for building others up according to their needs, that it may benefit those who listen" (Ephesians 4:29).

Overall, changing a critical spirit is a process that requires self-reflection, empathy, and a commitment to positive communication. As biblical counselors, we can help individuals overcome their critical spirit by identifying the root cause, fostering a culture of grace, developing empathy and compassion, and encouraging positive communication.

Identifying a Person with a Critical Spirit

A person with a critical spirit is characterized by fault-finding, negative attitudes, and harsh judgments. This individual is prone to complaining, seeing the glass as half-empty, whining about unmet expectations, predicting failure, and being judgmental. They tear down both others and their own well-being with this attitude.

"Beloved, do not believe every spirit, but test the spirits to see whether they are from God, for many false prophets have gone out into the world" (1 John 4:1).

Believers are commanded to "test the spirits to see whether they are from God." This command is echoed in other parts of Scripture as well. In 1 Thessalonians 5:20-21, Paul exhorts Christians to not "despise prophecies, but test everything; hold fast what is good." The test is to compare what is being taught with the clear teaching of the Bible. The Berean Jews were commended for examining the Scriptures daily to verify the teachings of Paul and Silas (Acts 17:10-11).

Traits of a Person with a Caring Spirit

A person with a caring spirit reflects the character of God, including His caring nature. "The Lord is good, a refuge in times of trouble. He cares for those who trust in him" (Nahum 1:7).

1. Empathy:

Able to put themselves in someone else's shoes and understand their feelings and struggles.

2. Compassion:

Feels deep compassion for others, wanting to help alleviate their pain.

3. Selflessness:

Thinks of others first and is willing to put their own needs aside to help others.

4. Kindness:

Treats others with respect and dignity.

5. Generosity:

Gives of their time, resources, and talents to help others in need.

6. Listening:

Takes the time to hear someone's story and understand their perspective.

7. Support:

Offers encouragement, comfort, and practical help when needed.

A caring person is attentive to another's dreams and disappointments, joys and sorrows, successes and failures, and vices and virtues. They have the heart of our Savior, Jesus Christ.

Contrasting a Critical Spirit with a Caring Spirit

a) A Critical Spirit: Condemns the person as well as the action.

A Caring Spirit: Condemns the action, not the person.

b) A Critical Spirit: Focuses on the faults of others.

A Caring Spirit: Focuses on self-examination.

c) A Critical Spirit: Ridicules others.

A Caring Spirit: Encourages others.

d) A Critical Spirit: Makes judgments based on appearances.

A Caring Spirit: Makes judgments based on facts.

e) A Critical Spirit: Assumes the worst without hearing from the accused.

A Caring Spirit: Assumes the best while hearing from the accused.

f) A Critical Spirit: Tears others down without seeing their unmet needs.

A Caring Spirit: Builds others up according to their needs.

g) A Critical Spirit: Responds harshly when criticized or accused.

A Caring Spirit: Responds appreciatively and seeks to correct personal misbehavior.

h) A Critical Spirit: Lacks mercy toward others.

A Caring Spirit: Responds with mercy toward others.

A critical spirit robs us of the ability to enjoy life and miss the beauty God has placed in this world.

Origins of a Critical Spirit

A critical spirit originates from a heart focused on self and lacking God's grace and forgiveness. "You have heard that it was said, 'Eye for an eye, and a tooth for a tooth.' But I tell you, do not resist an evil person. If anyone slaps you on the right cheek, turn to them the other cheek also" (Matthew 5:38-39).

It can stem from pride, fear, insecurity, and past hurts. Pride makes us think we are better than others, while fear and insecurity make us critical to protect ourselves. Past hurts can cause us to project our pain onto others, being overly harsh and judgmental.

Romans 12:1-2 and 2 Corinthians 10:5 remind us to transform our minds and take our thoughts captive. Philippians 4:8 encourages us to focus on what is true, honorable, just, pure, lovely, commendable, excellent, and praiseworthy.

Steps to Overcome a Critical Spirit

a) Identify Your Shortcomings:

"Search me, God, and know my heart; test me and know my anxious thoughts" (Psalm 139:23-24).

b) Practice Compassion for Others:

"Therefore, as God's chosen people, holy and dearly loved, clothe yourselves with compassion, kindness, humility, gentleness, and patience" (Colossians 3:12).

c) Draw Out the Heartfelt Needs of Others:

"The purposes of a person's heart are deep waters, but one who has insight draws them out" (Proverbs 20:5).

d) Offer Acceptance to Others:

"Accept one another, then, just as Christ accepted you, in order to bring praise to God" (Romans 15:7).

e) See the God-Given Worth in Others:

"Are not five sparrows sold for two pennies? Yet not one of them is forgotten by God. Indeed, the very hairs of your head are all numbered. Don't be afraid; you are worth more than many sparrows" (Luke 12:6-7).

f) Praise the Positive in Others:

"Finally, brothers and sisters, whatever is true, whatever is noble, whatever is right, whatever is pure, whatever is lovely, whatever is admirable—if anything is excellent or praiseworthy—think about such things" (Philippians 4:8).

g) Refuse to Wound Others with Words:

"Let the message of Christ dwell among you richly as you teach and admonish one another with all wisdom through psalms, hymns, and songs from the Spirit, singing to God with gratitude in your hearts" (Colossians 3:16).

h) See the Unmet Needs of Others:

"And my God will meet all your needs according to the riches of his glory in Christ Jesus" (Philippians 4:19).

i) Rely on God's Word and Spirit for Wisdom:

"This is what we speak, not in words taught us by human wisdom but in words taught by the Spirit, explaining spiritual realities with Spirit-taught words" (1 Corinthians 2:13).

Eradicating Judgmental Attitudes

Matthew

7:12, the "Golden Rule," states, "So in everything, do to others what you would have them do to you, for this sums up the Law and the Prophets." This principle calls us to treat others with the same respect, kindness, and generosity we would want for ourselves. It reflects God's love and compassion, transforming our attitudes and behaviors towards others.

Overcoming a critical spirit is a process of sanctification, aided by the Holy Spirit (2 Thessalonians 2:13). As we submit to God, read His Word, and pray for grace, we will find that the critical spirit gives way to the Holy Spirit's control, leading us to live with humility, grace, and selflessness.

CHAPTER 11
Cults: The Truth Twisters

"For such people are false apostles, deceitful workers, masquerading as apostles of Christ. And no wonder, for Satan himself masquerades as an angel of light. It is not surprising, then, if his servants also masquerade as servants of righteousness. Their end will be what their actions deserve." (2 Corinthians 11:13-15 NIV)

What is a Cult?

A cult is a sect or religious system that promotes doctrines deviating from orthodox biblical Christianity. Cults often revolve around a strong authoritarian leader who maintains strict control over the group's members through manipulation, indoctrination, and isolation from the outside world. Cults often have unique beliefs and practices that deviate from mainstream society and use deceptive tactics to recruit and retain members. While not all alternative or unconventional groups are cults, those using manipulative and harmful tactics should be avoided.

When people hear the word cult, they often think of groups worshiping Satan, sacrificing animals, or participating in bizarre, pagan rituals. However, a cult rarely involves such things. In its broadest sense, a cult is simply a religious system with particular rites and customs.

Fundamental Doctrines of the Christian Faith vs. Cults

Christianity has fundamental doctrines that cults often distort or deny. These doctrines can be remembered with the acronym V-A-R-I-E-S:

a) Virgin Birth: Jesus Christ was conceived by the Holy Spirit and born of the Virgin Mary (Matthew 1:18, 23).

b) Atonement: Only the shed blood of Jesus can pay the penalty for personal sin (Romans 5:8-9).

c) Resurrection: Jesus Christ was raised from the dead in bodily, physical form and was seen by many (1 Corinthians 15:3-6).

d) Incarnation: Jesus Christ, who is God, took on human form and was fully God and fully man (John 1:1-3, 14).

e) Eschatology: Jesus Christ will visibly return to earth during the end times, with a final judgment sending the unrighteous to eternal punishment and the righteous to eternal life (Matthew 25:46; Hebrews 9:27-28).

f) Scripture: The Bible is wholly inspired by God, without error in the original writings, and is the only authority for righteous living (Proverbs 30:5-6; 2 Timothy 3:16).

A cult teaches doctrines that, if believed, will cause a person to remain unsaved. A cult claims to be part of a religion yet denies essential truths of that religion. Therefore, a Christian cult will deny one or more fundamental truths of Christianity while still claiming to be Christian.

Characteristics of Cult Leaders

Cult leaders often present themselves as infallible authorities who require absolute loyalty. They persuade through their strong, charismatic personalities and prohibit individual freedom, demanding unquestioned obedience. They promote themselves as divine or as God's sole agent on earth, claiming to possess "new truth" while perverting biblical truth. They provide simplistic answers for complex problems.

Two of the most common teachings of cult leaders are that Jesus was not God and that salvation is not by faith alone. A denial of the deity of Christ results in the view that Jesus' death was insufficient to pay for our sins. A denial of salvation by faith alone results in the teaching that salvation is achieved by our own works. The Jehovah's Witnesses and Mormons are well-known examples, both denying the deity of Christ and salvation by faith alone.

Characteristics of Cult Followers

Followers of a cult typically follow their leader blindly, forfeiting individual freedom and often forsaking friends and family for a new "family." They fear punishment for not conforming to legalistic rules and regulations and feel misunderstood and persecuted by the outside world. They often forgo reason for emotion.

"Cult followers ... will not put up with sound doctrine. Instead, to suit their own desires, they will gather around them a great number of teachers to say what their itching ears want to hear" (2 Timothy 4:3).

Caring for Those in Cults

The captive's first need is to know they are respected as God's creation with God-given worth. Only then will they allow someone to plant seeds of doubt and replace false teaching with the Word of God.

Reaching Out Through Relationships

a) Show respect by taking time to listen.

b) Re-plant by sowing seeds of doubt.

c) Restore and regain what has been lost.

Guidelines for Reaching Out

a) Don't criticize or mock the cult leader and members.

b) Don't project negative emotions or argue, despite discomfort.

c) Don't interrupt, regardless of disapproval.

While it is wise to be prepared to defend the faith and have knowledge of false beliefs, neither alone will result in the conversion of those trapped in cults. The best we can do is pray for them, witness to them, and live the Christian life in front of them, trusting the Holy Spirit to draw, convince, and convert.

Sowing Seeds of Doubt

a) Plant the realization that joy exists outside the cult.

b) Plant-specific proof of cult errors.

c) Plant awareness that freedom to choose has been stifled.

d) Plant factual information about the cult.

e) Plant examples of inconsistencies within the cult's doctrinal teachings.

We must pray for those involved in cults, asking God to change their hearts and open their eyes to the truth (2 Corinthians 4:4). We should pray for their need for salvation through Jesus Christ (John 3:16) and rely on the power of God and conviction of the Holy Spirit to succeed in convincing anyone of the truth (John 16:7-11).

The Best Deterrent

Knowing biblical doctrine helps detect false teachings. "But examine everything carefully; hold fast to that which is good" (1 Thessalonians 5:21).

We should live a godly Christian life so those trapped in cults can see the change God has made in our lives (1 Peter 3:1-2). We must pray for wisdom in ministering to them effectively (James 1:5) and be bold in sharing the gospel (Romans 10:9-10). Always be prepared to defend the faith with gentleness and respect (1 Peter 3:15).

Steps to Freedom from a Cult

1. Educate Yourself: Research about the cult and its practices. "Then you will know the truth, and the truth will set you free" (John 8:32).

2. Find Support: Reach out to trusted friends, family members, or seek professional help. "Where there is no guidance, a people falls, but in an abundance of counselors there is safety" (Proverbs 11:14).

3. Plan Your Exit: Ensure you have a safe place and a support system in place. "The prudent see danger and take refuge, but the simple keep going and pay the penalty" (Proverbs 27:12).

4. Cut Ties: Sever all ties with the cult and its members. "Do not be misled: 'Bad company corrupts good character'" (1 Corinthians 15:33).

5. Seek Professional Help: Work with a trained mental health professional for support. "Plans fail for lack of counsel, but with many advisers, they succeed" (Proverbs 15:22).

Leaving a cult can be challenging, but with the right support and resources, it's possible to break free and live a fulfilling life outside the cult.

CHAPTER 12

Dating: The Delights and Dangers of Dating

"So they are no longer two, but one flesh. Therefore what God has joined together, let not man separate." (Matthew 19:6)

Delights of Dating

1. Building Relationships: Dating can be a great way to build relationships and connections with other people. It can be a fun way to get to know someone and see if you have a connection. Proverbs 27:17 says, "As iron sharpens iron, so one person sharpens another."

2. Learning About Yourself: Dating can also be an opportunity to learn about yourself and your preferences in a partner. You may discover new things about yourself and what you want in a relationship. James 1:5 reminds us, "If any of you lacks wisdom, you should ask God, who gives generously to all without finding fault, and it will be given to you."

3. Enjoying New Experiences: Dating can lead to new experiences and adventures, such as trying new restaurants, activities, or traveling to new places. Ecclesiastes 3:12-13 says, "I know that there is nothing better for people than to be happy and to do good while they live. That each of them may eat and drink and find satisfaction in all their toil—this is the gift of God."

4. Developing Communication Skills: Communication is key in any relationship, and dating can be a great way to develop your communication skills and learn how to express your thoughts and feelings. Ephesians 4:29 encourages us, "Do not let any unwholesome talk come out of your mouths, but only what is helpful for building others up according to their needs, that it may benefit those who listen."

Dangers of Dating

1. Emotional Vulnerability: Dating can make you emotionally vulnerable, which can lead to heartbreak and disappointment if the relationship doesn't work out. Proverbs 4:23 advises, "Above all else, guard your heart, for everything you do flows from it."

2. Risk of Being Taken Advantage Of: Unfortunately, there are people who use dating as a way to take advantage of others, such as scamming or manipulating them for personal gain. Matthew 10:16 warns, "I am sending you out like sheep among wolves. Therefore be as shrewd as snakes and as innocent as doves."

3. Physical Danger: Meeting someone new can also put you at risk for physical danger, such as assault or violence. Psalm 91:2 says, "I will say of the Lord, 'He is my refuge and my fortress, my God, in whom I trust.'"

4. Unhealthy Relationships: Dating can also lead to unhealthy relationships, such as those that are emotionally or physically abusive. 1 Corinthians 15:33 cautions, "Do not be misled: 'Bad company corrupts good character.'"

It's important to approach dating with caution and be aware of the potential risks, but also to enjoy the process and be open to new experiences. Remember to trust your instincts and prioritize your safety and well-being in any relationship.

The Ditch of Dating

Immorality is what soils a pure dating relationship. As Christians, we are called to be different in how we approach dating. Romans 12:2 says, "Do not conform to the pattern of this world, but be transformed by the renewing of your mind." The trend for dating today often involves several intimate romantic relationships before marriage. However, biblical dating aims for emotional and physical intimacy with only one person—your spouse.

Characteristics to Look for in a Prospective Date

1. Shared Values: It's important to find someone who shares your core values, such as honesty, loyalty, and respect. Amos 3:3 says, "Do two walk together unless they have agreed to do so?"

2. Emotional Intelligence: Look for someone who is emotionally intelligent and can communicate their feelings effectively. This can help build a deeper level of intimacy and connection in the relationship. Proverbs 25:11 states, "A word fitly spoken is like apples of gold in pictures of silver."

3. Compatibility: Find someone compatible with you in personality, interests, and lifestyle. 2 Corinthians 6:14 advises, "Do not be yoked together with unbelievers. For what do righteousness and wickedness have in common? Or what fellowship can light have with darkness?"

4. Kindness: Look for someone kind and compassionate towards others, indicating strong moral character and empathy. Ephesians 4:32 says, "Be kind and compassionate to one another, forgiving each other, just as in Christ God forgave you."

5. Respectful Behavior: Observe how your prospective date treats others, such as waitstaff or strangers. Look for someone who is respectful and considerate of others. Philippians 2:3-4 reminds us, "Do

nothing out of selfish ambition or vain conceit. Rather, in humility value others above yourselves, not looking to your own interests but each of you to the interests of the others."

Protecting Your Heart

When a dating friendship turns into a love relationship, protect your heart and remember that it belongs first to God. Proverbs 3:5-6 says, "Trust in the Lord with all your heart and lean not on your own understanding; in all your ways submit to him, and he will make your paths straight."

Do's and Don'ts of Dating

a) Don't Focus on Romance: Focus on building a solid friendship first. Proverbs 17:17 says, "A friend loves at all times, and a brother is born for a time of adversity."

b) Do Reflect Christian Values: Reflect Christian values on your date. Matthew 5:16 says, "In the same way, let your light shine before others, that they may see your good deeds and glorify your Father in heaven."

c) Don't Date Non-Christians: 2 Corinthians 6:14 warns, "Do not be yoked together with unbelievers."

d) Do Trust God's Plans: Trust in God's plans for your life. Jeremiah 29:11 says, "For I know the plans I have for you,' declares the Lord, 'plans to prosper you and not to harm you, plans to give you hope and a future."

Prayer of the Heart

Put God in charge of the timing and pace of your dating life. Psalm 37:5 says, "Commit your way to the Lord; trust in him, and he will do this."

Breaking Off a Dating Relationship

If someone asks how to break off a dating relationship, advise them to speak the truth in love (Ephesians 4:15). Make a clean break, respect the other person by speaking face-to-face, and be kind and clear in communication. Colossians 4:6 says, "Let your conversation be always full of grace, seasoned with salt, so that you may know how to answer everyone."

Handling a Breakup

If an individual is on the receiving end of a breakup, encourage them to listen, look at the big picture, and evaluate the reasons given. Philippians 4:6-7 advises, "Do not be anxious about anything, but in every situation, by prayer and petition, with thanksgiving, present your requests to God. And the peace of God, which transcends all understanding, will guard your hearts and your minds in Christ Jesus."

Maintaining Purity in a Dating Relationship

P-U-R-I-T-Y Acrostic:

a) Prioritize God's standard for purity: "But among you there must not be even a hint of sexual immorality, or of any kind of impurity, or of greed, because these are improper for God's holy people" (Ephesians 5:3).

b) Undertake personal accountability: "So then, each of us will give an account of ourselves to God" (Romans 14:12).

c) Refrain from activities that arouse sexual desires: "Flee from sexual immorality. All other sins a person commits are outside the body, but whoever sins sexually, sins against their own body" (1 Corinthians 6:18).

d) Implement goals that please God: "So whether you eat or drink or whatever you do, do it all for the glory of God" (1 Corinthians 10:31).

e) Trust in God's timing: "There is a time for everything, and a season for every activity under the heavens" (Ecclesiastes 3:1).

f) Yield your life to the Lord: "Submit yourselves, then, to God. Resist the devil, and he will flee from you" (James 4:7).

Scriptures for Pure Dating

1 Corinthians 6:9-7:19 (Command to be pure, seriousness of sexual sin, and instructions regarding marriage)

1 Thessalonians 4:1-8 (Do not wrong or defraud one another in relationships)

Song of Solomon 2:7 ("Do not awaken love before it pleases" — meaning marriage)

Proverbs 6:20-7:27 (Warning to avoid sexual sin and foolish relationships)

James 1:13-15 (Temptation is to be taken very seriously)

Romans 13:8-14 (Love others, work for their soul's good; don't look to please self)

Romans 14:1-15:7 (Favor others, not self; value what's good to their souls)

1 Timothy 5:1-2 (Treat single women as sisters in Christ, with absolute purity)

Titus 2:1-8 (Young men and women should focus on self-control/godliness)

John 14:15 ("If you love me, keep my commands.")

Overcoming the pitfalls of dating and maintaining purity requires God's wisdom and guidance. Let us seek His will and live according to His Word.

CHAPTER 13

Decision Making: Discerning the Will of God

"Do not merely listen to the Word and so deceive yourselves. Do what it says." (James 1:22)

The decision-making process is something that we all engage in every day of our lives. Some decisions are small, but others are very important to our well-being and even our salvation. Sometimes we make good decisions, and sometimes we make foolish decisions that can lead to destruction. Proverbs 3:5-6 advises, "Trust in the Lord with all your heart and lean not on your own understanding; in all your ways submit to him, and he will make your paths straight."

Steps to Discerning the Will of God

Discerning the will of God can be a challenging and complex process, as it often involves balancing our own desires and intentions with a desire to align ourselves with a higher power or divine plan. Here are some steps that may help in the process of discerning the will of God:

1. Seek Guidance: It can be helpful to seek guidance from spiritual leaders or mentors who can provide insight and support as you navigate your spiritual journey. Proverbs 15:22 says, "Plans fail for lack of counsel, but with many advisers, they succeed."

2. Pray and Meditate: Take time to pray and meditate, asking for guidance and clarity from God. This can help you connect with your inner wisdom and intuition. Philippians 4:6-7 encourages, "Do not be anxious about anything, but in every situation, by prayer and petition, with thanksgiving, present your requests to God. And the peace of God, which transcends all understanding, will guard your hearts and your minds in Christ Jesus."

3. Study Sacred Texts: Studying sacred texts, such as the Bible, can provide guidance and insight into God's will. Psalm 119:105 states, "Your word is a lamp for my feet, a light on my path."

4. Listen to Your Heart: Pay attention to your own desires and passions, as they may be indicators of God's will for your life. Listen to your heart and inner voice, and trust your intuition. Psalm 37:4 advises, "Take delight in the Lord, and he will give you the desires of your heart."

5. Practice Discernment: When making decisions, take time to discern and weigh the options, seeking guidance and insight from trusted sources. Romans 12:2 teaches, "Do not conform to the pattern of this world, but be transformed by the renewing of your mind. Then you will be able to test and approve what God's will is—his good, pleasing and perfect will."

6. Act with Faith: Once you have discerned God's will, act on it with faith and trust, knowing that you are following a divine plan for your life. Hebrews 11:6 reminds us, "And without faith, it is impossible to please God because anyone who comes to him must believe that he exists and that he rewards those who earnestly seek him."

Understanding God's Will

Has God Already Determined His Will for Me? (Ephesians 2:10): God's will has already been planned out for us, and how we will serve Him through good works is just as much a part of God's plan for us as who we should marry, where we should live, and what our career will be. These good works are valid evidence that someone is walking as one of God's chosen. Ephesians 2:10 says, "For we are God's handiwork, created in Christ Jesus to do good works, which God prepared in advance for us to do."

Can I Actually Know God's Will for My Life? (Acts 22:14): The idea of knowing God's will for your life is a common theme in many religious traditions. While some people believe that it is possible to discern God's will through prayer and contemplation, others believe that it is not always clear or straightforward. However, Ephesians 5:17 encourages us, "Therefore do not be foolish, but understand what the Lord's will is." Discerning God's specific will for our lives is a matter of wrestling with God in prayer and discovering how His general will ought to be worked out in our lives.

How Does God Reveal His Will? (John 16:13): God communicates His specific will to us through His Word and through prayer and fasting. He also speaks to us through His Spirit. John 16:13 says, "But when he, the Spirit of truth, comes, he will guide you into all the truth. He will not speak on his own; he will speak only what he hears, and he will tell you what is yet to come." Together, God's Word and His Spirit reveal what Jesus' will is.

Will God Reveal the Whole Blueprint of My Entire Life? (Psalm 32:8): God often reveals His will step by step rather than laying out the entire plan. Psalm 32:8 says, "I will instruct you and teach you in the way you should go; I will counsel you with my loving eye on you." Jeremiah 1:5 adds, "Before I formed you in the womb I knew you, before you were born I set you apart; I appointed you as a prophet to the nations."

Why Does God's Will for Me Sometimes Include Sorrow and Affliction? (Psalm 119:71): Suffering gives us compassion for others and allows us to see God's sufficiency as we learn to depend on Him. Romans 5:3-4 says, "Not only so, but we also glory in our sufferings because we know that suffering produces perseverance; perseverance, character; and character, hope."

God Blesses Decisions That:

1. He Initiates (Proverbs 4:11): "I instruct you in the way of wisdom and lead you along straight paths."

2. Line Up with His Word (Psalm 119:33): "Teach me, Lord, the way of your decrees, that I may follow it to the end."

3. Accomplish His Purpose (Philippians 2:13): "For it is God who works in you to will and to act in order to fulfill his good purpose."

4. Depend on His Strength (Philippians 4:13): "I can do all this through him who gives me strength."

5. Result in Giving Him Glory (1 Corinthians 10:31): "So whether you eat or drink or whatever you do, do it all for the glory of God."

6. Promote Justice, Kindness, and Humility (Micah 6:8): "He has shown you, O mortal, what is good. And what does the Lord require of you? To act justly and to love mercy and to walk humbly with your God."

7. Consider the Interests of Others (Philippians 2:4): "Not looking to your own interests but each of you to the interests of the others."

8. Are Bathed in Prayer (1 Thessalonians 5:17): "Pray continually."

Measuring Decisions by God's Standards

From God's perspective, decisions are not determined by random selection, supernatural events, people's opinions, delay tactics, analytical thinking, or good feelings. God wants us to measure our decisions by His standards. Ephesians 5:10 says, "Find out what pleases the Lord."

Seven Tests for Decision Making

When counseling those who are confused about decisions, lead them to test themselves against the following 7 tests:

1. Scriptural Test: Does the Bible endorse it? (Psalm 119:105)

2. Secrecy Test: Would it bother me if everyone knew this decision? (Luke 12:2-3)

3. Survey Test: What do wise counselors say about it? (Proverbs 15:22)

4. Spiritual Test: Am I being led by the Holy Spirit? (Romans 8:14)

5. Stumbling Test: Could this decision cause another person to stumble? (Romans 14:21)

6. Serenity Test: Do I have peace about it? (Philippians 4:6-7)

7. Sanctification Test: Will this decision make me more like Christ? (Romans 8:29)

Practical Guidance Using the Acronym G-U-I-D-A-N-C-E

Gifts: Consider how your God-given talents and abilities fit into your decision. (Romans 12:6)

Understanding: Seek God's wisdom and understanding. (Proverbs 3:5-6)

Impressions: Be open to the Holy Spirit's leading. (John 16:13)

Desires: Align your desires with God's will. (Psalm 37:4)

Advice: Seek counsel from godly advisors. (Proverbs 11:14)

Necessity: Determine the necessity of the decision. (Philippians 4:19)

Circumstances: Evaluate your circumstances in light of God's Word. (Romans 8:28)

Elimination: Eliminate options that contradict God's Word. (Ephesians 5:10)

Praying for Wisdom

When time has run out and you still do not know what to do, pray and ask God for wisdom. James 1:5 says, "If any of you lacks wisdom, you should ask God, who gives generously to all without finding fault, and it will be given to you." God wants us to learn how to make good decisions. The next time you need to make a big decision, consider praying for wisdom and seeking God's guidance in every step.

CHAPTER 14

Depression: Walking from Darkness into the Dawn

"Why are you downcast, oh my soul? Why so disturbed within me? Put your hope in God, for I will yet praise Him, my Savior, my God." (Psalm 42:5)

Depression is a psychological condition that affects the whole person—body, soul, and spirit. It generates a sense of hopelessness and has two primary characteristics: heavy hearts and sustained sadness. Depression is not merely feeling down; it is a mental health disorder characterized by persistent feelings of sadness, hopelessness, and/or loss of interest in activities that used to bring pleasure. It affects a person's thoughts, feelings, behavior, and overall functioning.

Understanding Depression

Depression can vary in severity and duration, and some people may experience it only once in their lifetime, while others may have recurring episodes. Symptoms of depression can include:

- Persistent feelings of sadness, anxiety, or emptiness (Psalm 34:18)

- Loss of interest or pleasure in activities once enjoyed (Ecclesiastes 3:1-8)

- Fatigue or lack of energy (Isaiah 40:31)

- Difficulty concentrating or making decisions (James 1:5)

- Sleep disturbances (insomnia or oversleeping) (Psalm 127:2)

- Changes in appetite and weight (Psalm 107:9)

- Feelings of worthlessness or guilt (Romans 8:1)

- Thoughts of suicide or death (Psalm 31:9)

Depression is a treatable condition, and there are several effective treatment options available, including therapy, medication, and lifestyle changes. It's important to seek help from a mental health professional if you are experiencing symptoms of depression (Psalm 34:17).

Recognizing the Reality of Depression

Some people describe depression as "living in a black hole" or having a feeling of impending doom. Others feel lifeless, empty, and apathetic. Just getting through the day can be overwhelming. Feeling down from time to time is a normal part of life, but when emotions such as hopelessness and despair take hold and just won't go away, a person may be suffering from depression. Depression makes it tough to function and enjoy life like they once did. But the Bible tells us how we can get through this.

Causes of Depression

Depression is not a result of sin when a person:

- Grieves over normal losses (Ecclesiastes 3:4)

- Experiences natural deterioration due to the passing of years (2 Corinthians 4:16)

Depression can be a result of sin when a person:

- Suffers the consequences of sinful choices yet continues without change (Romans 6:23)

- Doesn't take necessary steps for healing, such as seeking biblical counseling, memorizing Scripture, reading Christian materials, and getting medical help when appropriate (Proverbs 19:20)

- Holds on to self-pity, anger, and bitterness instead of choosing to forgive (Ephesians 4:31-32)

- Uses depression to manipulate others (Philippians 2:3)

- Continually chooses to blame God and others for their unhappiness (Romans 9:20)

- Allows others to control them instead of choosing to obey Christ and letting Him be in control (Galatians 1:10)

Symptoms of Depression

Depressed persons often display sad, discouraged, joyless dispositions. Major depressive episodes often involve five or more of the following classic symptoms nearly every day for at least two weeks:

- Pervasive depressed mood (Psalm 42:11)

- Diminished pleasure in usual activities (Ecclesiastes 2:1-11)

- Significant change in appetite or weight (Psalm 107:9)

- Fatigue or loss of energy (Isaiah 40:29-31)

- Diminished ability to think clearly, evaluate, or concentrate (James 1:5)

- Suicidal thoughts or attempts (Psalm 31:12)

Addressing Physical Contributors to Depression

Various physical conditions may contribute to depression, such as biochemical imbalances that can be treated successfully with medication. Taking medication for depression does not mean a person lacks faith. Ezekiel 47:12 explains that God made leaves for healing. Medication should never be used to numb pain or escape it, but to help the person process the pain. Medication should be the last avenue, tried only after all other steps have been taken, and always in conjunction with biblical counsel for healing.

Emotional Contributors to Depression

Three emotional contributors to depression include:

- Loss (Job 1:21)

- Fear (Isaiah 41:10)

- Stress (Philippians 4:6-7)

Depression is more than just a bad mood. Often, a faith-based counselor can assist depressed individuals by helping them uncover life problems contributing to their depression, identify destructive thinking that makes them feel hopeless, and explore any behaviors or self-talk magnifying their depression. Even our deep disappointments must be resolved, or our bitterness will cause trouble (Hebrews 12:15).

Spiritual Contributors to Depression

Two spiritual contributors of depression include:

- Disobedience (1 Samuel 15:22-23)

- Guilt (Psalm 32:1-5)

Like the disobedient Israelites, a person will find depression sweeping over them unless they apply the remedy of confession and repentance: a change of mind and a change of direction (Deuteronomy 28:65).

Steps to C-O-N-Q-U-E-R Depression

C: Confront any loss in your life, allowing yourself to grieve and be healed (Psalm 34:18).

O: Offer your heart to God for cleansing and confess your sins (1 John 1:9).

N: Nurture thoughts that focus on God's great love for you (Jeremiah 31:3).

Q: Quit negative thinking and negative self-talk (Philippians 4:8).

U: Understand God's eternal purpose for allowing personal loss and heartache (Romans 8:28).

E: Exchange your hurt and anger for thanksgiving (1 Thessalonians 5:18).

R: Remember that God is sovereign over your life, and He promises hope for your future (Jeremiah 29:11).

Biblical Counseling to Overcome Depression

Below is a list of just a few ways a biblical counselor might help another person out of the "ditch of depression.":

- Learn all you can about depression—read books, watch videos, attend seminars (Proverbs 18:15).

- If suicide is a concern, ask, "Are you thinking about hurting yourself or taking your life?" (Proverbs 24:11-12).

- Take all suicide and self-injury threats seriously (Psalm 31:22).

- Be an accountability partner and say, "I am with you in this, and I won't abandon you" (Ecclesiastes 4:9-10).

- Help your client set goals, ensuring they understand the difference between a goal and a wish (Habakkuk 2:2).

Goal Setting

Encourage a depressed counselee to make a goal list. Habakkuk 2:2 says, "And the Lord answered me, and said, Write the vision, and make it plain upon tables, that he may run that readeth it." The list should include immediate goals, goals for the next three months, goals for the year, and looking ahead to the next five years. God said we should make our goal list "plain." That means making it practical so, when we read it, we can see the steps needed to make it happen.

CHAPTER 15

Domestic Violence: Assault on a Woman's Worth

"He who brings trouble on his family will inherit only wind, and the fool will be servant to the wise." (Proverbs 11:29)

Understanding Domestic Violence

Domestic violence is a pattern of abusive behavior in any intimate or familial relationship where one person tries to gain power and control over the other person through physical, emotional, sexual, or financial abuse. It can occur between spouses or partners, parents, and children, siblings, or any other family member. Domestic violence can take many forms, including physical violence, emotional abuse, financial abuse, sexual abuse, and isolation. It is a serious problem that can have long-term consequences for the victim's physical and mental health, and it is important to seek help if you or someone you know is experiencing domestic violence.

The Reality of Domestic Violence

Domestic violence refers to a pattern of coercive and violent behavior exercised by one adult in an intimate relationship with another. Approximately 95% of domestic violence victims are women. Many of these women blame themselves for the abuse, which further fuels the cycle of violence. The violation of a trusted relationship produces severe pain as the individual often tries to escape, only to be pushed back to suffer more abuse. In the midst of it all, the abuse victim can find comfort in the Word of God: "The Lord is close to the brokenhearted and saves those who are crushed in spirit" (Psalm 34:18).

The Cycle of Abuse

Abusive patterns in domestic violence develop in three stages which are cyclical and become increasingly violent. Here are the U.S. national statistics on domestic violence, compiled by the National Coalition Against Domestic Violence:

- On average, nearly 20 people per minute are physically abused by an intimate partner in the United States. During one year, this equates to more than 10 million women and men.

- 1 in 3 women and 1 in 4 men have been victims of some form of physical violence by an intimate partner within their lifetime.

- 1 in 4 women and 1 in 7 men have been victims of severe physical violence by an intimate partner in their lifetime.

- 1 in 7 women and 1 in 18 men have been stalked by an intimate partner to the point where they felt very fearful or believed that they or someone close to them would be harmed or killed.

- On a typical day, there are more than 20,000 phone calls placed to domestic violence hotlines nationwide.

- The presence of a gun in a domestic violence situation increases the risk of homicide by 500%.

- Intimate partner violence accounts for 15% of all violent crime.

- Women between the ages of 18-24 are most commonly abused by an intimate partner.

- 19% of domestic violence involves a weapon.

- Domestic victimization is correlated with a higher rate of depression and suicidal behavior.

- Only 34% of people who are injured by intimate partners receive medical care for their injuries.

The Impact of Domestic Violence

Most people find it difficult to grasp these statistics. They wonder, "Why does he do it? Why does she put up with it? Why doesn't she just leave?" Strong emotional and psychological forces keep the victim tied to the abuser. Sometimes situational realities like a lack of money keep the victim from leaving. The reasons for staying vary from one victim to the next and usually involve several factors. As counselors, we need to explore the reasons for staying. Family members who fall victim to these patterns can feel traumatized by the mere anticipation of a violent eruption. The escalating nature of abuse is rarely curbed without intervention and adequate accountability. "Break the arm of the wicked and evil man; call him to account for his wickedness that would not be found out" (Psalm 10:15).

The Stages of Abuse

1. The Acute Stage:

During this stage, the pressure becomes so intense that the abuser erupts and gives full vent to their rage. The behavior of the abuser becomes so intense that others need to be called in to diffuse this rage, and often the police may need to be involved. "Rescue me, O Lord, from evil men; protect me from men of violence" (Psalm 140:1).

2. The Apologetic Stage:

During this stage, also known as the honeymoon phase, the abuser becomes contrite and attempts to soothe the victim with loving actions. This temporary phase is characterized by a dramatic transformation from being villainous to virtuous, including apologies, gifts, crying, promises, romance, and even accepting responsibility. The victim often has renewed hope for change and extends forgiveness. "A gentle answer turns away wrath, but a harsh word stirs up anger" (Proverbs 15:1).

3. The Agitated Stage:

During this stage, the abuser communicates dissatisfaction and blames their partner, maintaining passive psychological control and creating a fear of impending disaster. The victim tends to accept responsibility for the abuser's unhappiness and adjusts their behavior in an effort to please the abuser and relieve tension in the home. "He who covers over an offense promotes love, but whoever repeats the matter separates close friends" (Proverbs 17:9).

The Root Causes and Misunderstandings

The root cause of domestic violence and all the encompassing 'whys' often lie within the heart of every person. There are three God-given inner needs: love, significance, and security. In domestic violence, the abuser who abuses to feel significant believes that his partner is to blame for what is happening. If he doesn't attempt to control her, he fears losing her. "Each one should test his own actions. Then he can take pride in himself, without comparing himself to somebody else" (Galatians 6:4).

The abused often feels she is to blame for the violence; therefore, she continues trying to please him to be secure, no matter how bad it gets. Although these inner needs are sometimes met illegitimately, both the abuser and the abused may act or react to get these needs met. "Humble yourselves before the Lord, and he will lift you up" (James 4:10).

Misconceptions about Submission and Abuse

The abused may have an incorrect understanding of biblical submission and believe that enduring abuse is normal. She may also fear leaving because of threats from the abuser or because she believes any father for her children is better than no father. The Bible teaches that wives are to submit to their husbands, but it does not condone staying in an abusive relationship. "Wives, submit to your husbands as to the Lord... Husbands, love your wives, just as Christ loved the church and gave himself up for her" (Ephesians 5:22-25). Physical violence against a spouse is immoral and should not be tolerated. "The Lord examines the righteous, but the wicked and those who love violence his soul hates" (Psalm 11:5).

Practical Steps and Safety Planning

Some practical steps to help those caught in domestic violence include nurturing healthy boundaries that will help to curtail codependent habits and eventually put them on the road to transformation, where Christ-like maturity protects and takes mastery over their relationships:

B-O-U-N-D-A-R-I-E-S:

B: Begin a new way of thinking about yourself, God, and abuse (Romans 12:2).

O: Overcome fear of the unknown by trusting God with the future (Jeremiah 29:11).

U: Understand the biblical mandate to hold abusers accountable (Proverbs 27:5).

N: Notify others of your needs (Supportive friends, relatives, or others) (Galatians 6:2).

D: Develop God's perspective on biblical submission (Ephesians 5:21-33).

A: Admit your anger and practice forgiveness (Ephesians 4:26-27).

R: Recognize your codependent patterns of relating and change your response (Galatians 1:10).

I: Identify healthy boundaries for yourself and commit to maintaining them (Proverbs 4:23).

E: Ensure your personal safety (and the safety of your children) immediately (Psalm 121:7-8).

S: See your identity as being a precious child of God through your belief in Jesus Christ, and understand that your identity is in Him rather than your role as a spouse (Galatians 3:26).

Seeking Help and God's Guidance

If you are in an abusive relationship, it is crucial to seek help and ensure your safety. Know that God does not want you to remain in that situation. It is not God's will for you to accept physical, sexual, or psychological abuse. Leave the situation, find someone to help you stay safe, and involve law enforcement immediately. Through it all, pray for God's guidance and protection. "The Lord is a refuge for the oppressed, a stronghold in times of trouble" (Psalm 9:9).

CHAPTER 16

Dysfunctional Family: Making Peace with Your Past

"Shall we accept good from God, and not trouble?" (Job 2:10)

A dysfunctional family is a family unit in which relationships and interactions between family members are characterized by a variety of unhealthy patterns, such as conflict, neglect, abuse, or lack of communication. These families may also lack appropriate boundaries, rules, and structure, leading to a lack of stability and predictability within the family system. Dysfunctional families can cause emotional, psychological, and physical distress, significantly impacting the mental health and well-being of their members. They can also lead to negative behaviors, such as substance abuse, addiction, or self-harm. It's crucial to understand that while every family faces challenges, dysfunctional families persistently exhibit patterns that cause significant harm.

Characteristics of Dysfunctional Families

Dysfunctional families often exhibit traits such as alcoholism or substance abuse, emotional or physical abuse, lack of emotional support or empathy, poor communication or conflict resolution skills, enmeshment or over-involvement in each other's lives, triangulation (involving a third person in family conflicts), and denial of problems or avoidance of conflict. These patterns persist over time and significantly impact the well-being of family members.

The Bible emphasizes the importance of healthy relationships and communication within families: "Fathers, do not embitter your children, or they will become discouraged" (Colossians 3:21).

Types of Dysfunctional Parents

Passive Parent:

A passive parent allows inappropriate behavior to continue without establishing boundaries, to the detriment of other family members. Passive parents tend to make excuses for their children's behavior, rationalizing it rather than addressing the underlying causes.

Problem Parent:

A problem parent engages in immature, inappropriate, or destructive behavior, negatively affecting other family members. This behavior can include substance abuse, emotional instability, or abusive tendencies.

The Bible advises against such parental negligence and misconduct: "Discipline your children, and they will give you peace; they will bring you the delights you desire" (Proverbs 29:17).

Types of Children in Dysfunctional Families

The Clown:

This child uses humor and antics to divert attention away from family problems. Often hyperactive, this child seeks to be the center of attention.

The Scapegoat:

This child draws focus away from family problems through rebellious and uncontrollable behavior, consuming the family's time and energy and often developing self-destructive patterns.

The Lost Child:

This child hopes that by ignoring family problems, they will go away. They avoid attention and are often lonely and withdrawn.

The Hero:

This child tries to fix family problems and create a positive family image through noteworthy achievements, often developing perfectionistic and compulsive behaviors.

The Bible reminds us that every child is unique and valuable: "Train up a child in the way he should go; even when he is old he will not depart from it" (Proverbs 22:6).

Types of Dysfunctional Families

Chaotic Family:

Children in chaotic families, especially those with an alcoholic parent, may become super responsible with tendencies toward perfectionism or, conversely, super irresponsible when their attempts at perfectionism fall short.

Controlling Family:

In controlling families, one or more members exert excessive control over others, often stifling individuality and growth.

Coddling Family:

Coddling parents prevent children from learning independence and problem-solving skills, resulting in emotionally dependent adults.

Codependent Family:

Codependent families exhibit unhealthy dependence on each other. For instance, parents may rely excessively on their grown children, reversing the parent-child dynamic.

Healthy boundaries are essential for functional family relationships: "But let each one test his own work, and then his reason to boast will be in himself alone and not in his neighbor" (Galatians 6:4).

Characteristics of Functional Families

Functional families maintain structure and discipline, require individual responsibility, foster love and obedience to God, and create a secure environment for children. Each family member has a role to play in God's plan for the family, as described by Paul: "Submit to one another out of reverence for Christ" (Ephesians 5:21). Open communication and mutual respect are essential for maintaining a healthy family dynamic.

Suggestions for Parents Recognizing Dysfunctional Patterns

For parents acknowledging their role in family dysfunction, the following steps can help initiate healing and transformation:

Grieve Your Past:

Allow yourself to process and grieve your past mistakes and experiences.

Give Up Control:

Relinquish the need to control every aspect of your family's life, trusting God's plan instead.

Put Christ First:

Prioritize your relationship with Christ, allowing His love and guidance to influence your actions.

Give Thanks:

Express gratitude for your past experiences, recognizing how they have shaped you and your family.

"Trust in the Lord with all your heart and lean not on your own understanding; in all your ways submit to him, and he will make your paths straight" (Proverbs 3:5-6).

Cultivating Healthy Relationships

To cultivate healthy relationships within a dysfunctional family, biblical counselors can encourage the following:

Emphasize Uniqueness:

Recognize and celebrate the individuality of each family member (1 Corinthians 12:14-17).

Seek Togetherness and Individuality:

Foster a balance between family unity and individual growth (1 Corinthians 12:4-7).

Maintain Consistency:

Ensure consistent and clear communication (James 3:10-13).

Allow for Mistakes:

Provide grace and forgiveness for mistakes (Ephesians 4:32).

Encourage Emotional Expression:

Promote healthy and appropriate expression of feelings (Proverbs 20:5).

Develop Talents:

Support the development of natural talents and abilities (Proverbs 22:6).

Responsibility:

Encourage accountability for actions and attitudes (Galatians 6:4-5).

Treat with Love and Respect:

Show love and respect to all family members (1 Corinthians 16:14).

Depend on the Lord:

Cultivate a reliance on God for guidance and support (Proverbs 3:5-6).

By fostering these healthy practices, families can move from dysfunction towards wholeness and healing, relying on God's guidance and strength.

CHAPTER 17

Does God Cause Evil and Suffering?

The question of whether God causes evil and suffering is a complex and deeply philosophical one that has been debated for centuries. Many religious traditions hold that God is all-powerful, all-knowing, and perfectly good, and yet evil and suffering continue to exist in the world. This has led to a variety of theological explanations and debates. The Bible acknowledges this complexity and offers insight into God's nature and human suffering.

Free Will and Suffering

One perspective is that God allows evil and suffering to exist in the world because of free will. In this view, humans are given the ability to make choices, and some of these choices lead to evil and suffering. God respects our free will and allows us to make our own choices, even when those choices lead to negative consequences. The Bible supports this view: "See, I set before you today life and prosperity, death and destruction" (Deuteronomy 30:15).

Suffering for a Greater Purpose

Another perspective is that evil and suffering are part of God's plan for the world, serving a greater purpose. Suffering can lead to personal growth, spiritual development, or the cultivation of virtues such as compassion and empathy. Romans 5:3-4 tells us, "Not only so, but we also glory in our sufferings, because we know that suffering produces perseverance; perseverance, character; and character, hope."

Natural Suffering

However, it's also important to acknowledge that some forms of suffering, such as natural disasters or diseases, are not the result of human choices and may not serve an obvious purpose. These types of suffering can be especially challenging to understand from a theological perspective. The Bible reflects this struggle, as seen in the Book of Job, where Job questions why he suffers despite his righteousness (Job 1-2).

The Fairness of God

"God has not given us a spirit of fear, but of power and of love and of a sound mind" (2 Timothy 1:7). Nowhere in Scripture is the fairness of God questioned more profoundly than in the Book of Job. Job recognized that God does not owe us good; He gives it as a gift that we should accept. Accordingly, if adversity comes to us, we will be wise to see that even in adversity, there may be a gift that we should accept.

God's Identification with Our Suffering

To answer the questions, "Why should I believe in a God who allows evil?" and "Does God really care that I am hurting?" we can look to God's actions. God willingly suffered to identify with us and to save us. "But He was pierced for our transgressions, He was crushed for our iniquities; the punishment that brought us peace was on Him, and by His wounds, we are healed" (Isaiah 53:5).

The Role of Pain and Suffering

Pain can weaken our resistance and make everything look and feel worse than it really is. Satan knows this can be an Achilles heel and likes to use it against us. But Jesus is our perfect example. He willingly endured the pain and suffering of His death on the Cross because He loves us and wants us to be with Him forever in heaven. "For the joy set before Him, He endured the cross, scorning its shame, and sat down at the right hand of the throne of God" (Hebrews 12:2).

The Existence of Evil

"Couldn't God have made a world without evil?" (Revelation 20:1, 3). Yes, however, God knew that a world of limited moral freedom would actually be an inferior world because virtues are defined by their opposites. Evil is based on moral right and wrong choices.

God's Sovereignty and Human Choice

If God is all-good and all-powerful, why doesn't He anticipate evil and stop it? "The Lord is upright; He is my Rock, and there is no wickedness in Him" (Psalm 92:15). Evil and its effects of pain and suffering are present in the world today from the initial sin and disobedience of Adam and Eve. People continue to exert their God-given free will and disobey God by choice. "For all have sinned and fall short of the glory of God" (Romans 3:23).

Why God Allows Suffering

God sometimes causes suffering to bring about the greater good. Suffering is intrinsically related to the fallenness of this world. There was no suffering prior to sin. The fact is, if there were no sin in this world today, there would be no suffering. God allows suffering as part of His judgment, but He also uses it for our redemption — to shape our character and build up our faith. "Consider it pure joy, my brothers and sisters, whenever you face trials of many kinds, because you know that the testing of your faith produces perseverance" (James 1:2-3).

God's Omniscience and Our Prayers

God knows all our needs even before we ask and He hears all our prayers and answers. His answer may be 'yes' or 'no', but sometimes it is 'wait'. "The righteous cry out, and the Lord hears them; He delivers them from all their troubles" (Psalm 34:17-19).

Purposeful Suffering

Although suffering is a result of fallen humanity, God's highest purpose is to use it to conform us to the image of Christ in all we do and speak. "And we know that in all things God works for the good of those who love Him, who have been called according to His purpose" (Romans 8:28).

Understanding Suffering

In understanding why God allows suffering in our life, we understand that God is not powerless concerning our suffering but purposeful. "For I know the plans I have for you," declares the Lord, "plans to prosper you and not to harm you, plans to give you hope and a future" (Jeremiah 29:11).

God's Guidance

God has given us His Word to address the reasons for His purpose in allowing pain and suffering. "In the beginning was the Word, and the Word was with God, and the Word was God" (John 1:1).

Ways God Uses Suffering

God uses suffering to expose our sins, build our character, produce much good, change our perspective, and bless our future. "Not only so, but we also glory in our sufferings, because we know that suffering produces perseverance; perseverance, character; and character, hope" (Romans 5:3-4).

God's Care and Compassion

God cares deeply about our suffering, as demonstrated by the following facts:

- He encamps around you in the midst of trouble. "The angel of the Lord encamps around those who fear Him, and He delivers them" (Psalm 34:7).

- He is near you when you are brokenhearted. "The Lord is close to the brokenhearted and saves those who are crushed in spirit" (Psalm 34:18).

- He keeps a record of your grief and puts your tears in His bottle. "Record my misery; list my tears on your scroll—are they not in your record?" (Psalm 56:8).

In conclusion, while the existence of evil and suffering is a profound and challenging issue, the Bible provides us with insights and assurances that God is both just and compassionate. He allows suffering for purposes beyond our understanding but also promises His presence and ultimate redemption through Christ.

CHAPTER 18

Fear: No Longer Afraid

"Who have been robbed of the truth and who think that godliness is a means of financial gain." (1 Timothy 6:5)

Understanding Fear

Fear is an emotional response to a perceived threat or danger. It is a natural and instinctive response that helps humans and animals avoid danger and protect themselves. When we experience fear, our body responds with a series of physical and mental reactions, including an increased heart rate, rapid breathing, sweating, and heightened alertness. The Bible speaks to our fears, reminding us of God's presence and power: "For God has not given us a spirit of fear, but of power and of love and of a sound mind" (2 Timothy 1:7).

Types of Fear

There are many different types of fear, including:

1. Realistic Fear - A fear that is based on a real and immediate threat, such as the fear of falling from a great height.

2. Irrational Fear - A fear that is not based on a real or immediate threat, such as the fear of spiders.

3. Phobia - An intense and irrational fear of a specific object, situation, or activity, such as a fear of flying or heights.

4. Anxiety - A feeling of unease, such as worry or nervousness, that can be caused by a variety of factors, including fear.

While fear can be a helpful response in certain situations, it can also become excessive or overwhelming, leading to anxiety or other mental health issues. In some cases, fear can also be irrational or unfounded, and may require professional help to manage. The Bible reassures us: "Do not be anxious about anything, but in every situation, by prayer and petition, with thanksgiving, present your requests to God" (Philippians 4:6).

The Nature of Fear

Fear is a strong emotional reaction to imminent danger, whether real or imagined, rational or irrational, normal or abnormal. It includes a strong desire to escape the situation. People who experience an abnormally high amount of fear often feel overwhelmed, immobilized, and unable to make decisions about what to do to overcome the threat of danger. Fear acts as a protective device, placed in us by our Creator to alert all our physical systems when we are faced with real danger. Proverbs 3:25-26 reminds us, "Do not be afraid of sudden terror, nor of trouble from the wicked when it comes; For the Lord will be your confidence, and will keep your foot from being caught."

Identifying and Resolving Fear

The strategy that can help a person resolve their fear is to go before God, who is a source of wisdom, and pray from the heart. After seeking God's guidance, the individual needs to specifically identify their fears, listing exactly what they are afraid of. They should then ask themselves the following questions (Proverbs 14:8):

a) Is my fear tied to recent events, or did it originate from some specific situation in the past?

b) Is the object or occasion of my fear a true threat or merely a perceived threat?

Some people are never able to make the distinction between real threats and imagined ones. Job 3:25 states, "What I feared has come upon me; what I dreaded has happened to me."

Overcoming Fear

If a person grew up in a home where fear reigned, they may have developed a fear-based mentality and grown into an adult controlled by fear. Four ways to overcome fear when facing a person or situation include:

a) Ask Yourself If What You Fear Is Actually Likely to Happen - Manufactured fear is often about what "could" happen.

b) Realize That Fixation on Fear Guarantees Its Repetition - Fixation on fear ensures it will continue to dominate your thoughts.

c) Understand That Most Fear Has Nothing to Do with What Is Happening Now - Fear is often rooted in past experiences.

d) Determine How Current the Fear Is That You Are Presently Feeling - Assess whether your fear is relevant to the present situation.

The Bible encourages us to "be strong and courageous. Do not be afraid or terrified because of them, for the Lord your God goes with you; he will never leave you nor forsake you" (Deuteronomy 31:6).

Replacing Fear with Faith

In replacing fear with faith on the path to recovery and moving onto the Road to Transformation, it begins with a healthy fear or awe of God. The Bible tells us, "The fear of the Lord is the beginning of wisdom" (Proverbs 9:10). Believe that:

a) God Created You Because He Loves You - "I have loved you with an everlasting love; I have drawn you with unfailing kindness" (Jeremiah 31:3).

b) God Has a Purpose and Plan for Your Life - "For I know the plans I have for you," declares the Lord, "plans to prosper you and not to harm you, plans to give you hope and a future" (Jeremiah 29:11).

c) God Has the Right to Have Authority Over You - "Submit yourselves, then, to God. Resist the devil, and he will flee from you" (James 4:7).

d) God Wants You to Entrust Your Life to Him - "Commit your way to the Lord; trust in him and he will do this" (Psalm 37:5).

e) God Will Keep Your Mind Safe as You Trust in Him - "You will keep in perfect peace those whose minds are steadfast because they trust in you" (Isaiah 26:3).

f) God Has the Power to Change You - "Therefore, if anyone is in Christ, the new creation has come: The old has gone, the new is here!" (2 Corinthians 5:17).

Living Without Fear

Living in a state of fear is NOT God's plan for you, because fear-based thinking is not trusting God, not appropriating the grace of God, keeping you in bondage to fear, and physically, emotionally, and spiritually damaging. Psalm 91:1-2 reassures us, "Whoever dwells in the shelter of the Most High will rest in the shadow of the Almighty. I will say of the Lord, 'He is my refuge and my fortress, my God, in whom I trust.'"

Practical Steps to Overcoming Fear

In replacing fear with faith, your clients must be willing to analyze their fear honestly to discover its real source, whether it is rejection, failure, or financial loss. They must also be committed to developing their faith in the Lord by being:

a) Active in a Bible study.

b) In daily prayer, truly talking with God.

c) Committed to memorizing and meditating on God's Word.

d) Obedient to God's promptings in their spirit.

Facing Fear with Faith

Your clients must be willing to face their situations with faith and the power of Christ, by:

a) Knowing Christ is always ready to respond.

b) Acknowledging His actual presence and seeking His help.

c) Giving their fear to Him and receiving His powerful love.

d) Acting in love toward others by focusing on their needs.

God doesn't promise to always take away all our fears. Yet He gives us the power, love, and self-discipline necessary to embrace His life-changing truth. "For the Spirit God gave us does not make us timid, but gives us power, love and self-discipline" (2 Timothy 1:7).

Suggestions for Biblical Counselors

Here are some 'Don'ts' for the biblical counselor that may help others to overcome their fears:

a) Don't become impatient when you don't understand the person's fear.

b) Don't think the person is doing this for attention.

c) Don't be critical or use demeaning statements.

d) Don't assume you know what is best.

e) Don't make a person face a threatening situation without planning.

f) Don't make the person face the situation alone.

Conquering Fear with Faith

The greater our fear, the less we are controlled by faith. The greater our faith, the less we are controlled by fear. Isaiah 41:10 encourages us, "So do not fear, for I am with you; do not be dismayed, for I am your God. I will strengthen you and help you; I will uphold you with my righteous right hand."

Years ago, I had a personal problem with fear. I couldn't sleep at night, imagining the worst. To overcome this, I began a collection of "fear not" verses, which I copied into a journal and reviewed daily. My children also got involved, and I would find Bible verses written in a childish hand on a smudged paper. There were about 75 passages in the journal when it disappeared. Someone must have taken that journal who needed to read that wonderful message from God: "Fear not, for I will help you. Fear not, for I am with you." By the time the journal disappeared, I had internalized the message. Praise God, fear is no longer a dominating emotion in my life. That is the power in the Word of God.

CHAPTER 19

Financial Freedom: The Dollar Dilemma

"Who have been robbed of the truth and who think that godliness is a means of financial gain." (1 Timothy 6:5)

Understanding Financial Freedom

Financial freedom refers to a state where an individual or household has sufficient savings, assets, and passive income to cover their living expenses and financial goals without relying on traditional employment income. Achieving financial freedom means having enough resources to support your desired lifestyle and achieve financial objectives without the need to work for a living. The Bible teaches us the importance of managing our resources wisely: "The plans of the diligent lead surely to abundance, but everyone who is hasty comes only to poverty" (Proverbs 21:5).

The Path to Financial Freedom

Financial freedom provides individuals with greater control over their lives and allows them to pursue passions and interests without financial constraints. It offers a sense of security and stability, equipping them to handle unexpected expenses or emergencies. However, achieving financial freedom requires discipline, planning, and consistent effort over time. It is not a quick fix or a one-size-fits-all solution, and the path may differ for each individual. Jesus emphasized the importance of thoughtful planning and wise stewardship in the parable of the talents (Matthew 25:14-30).

Misconceptions About Wealth

There is a common misconception that achieving wealth is inherently unchristian or that money itself is evil. The Bible clarifies that it is the love of money, not money itself, that is the root of all evil (1 Timothy 6:10). The love of money can lead to behaviors that are contrary to godliness, such as lying, stealing, cheating, gambling, and even murder. Ecclesiastes 5:10 echoes this sentiment: "Whoever loves money never has enough; whoever loves wealth is never satisfied with their income."

Money and Contentment

Many believe that having more money will bring satisfaction, but Solomon, one of the wealthiest men in history, knew otherwise. He wrote, "Whoever loves money never has enough; whoever loves wealth is never satisfied with their income" (Ecclesiastes 5:10). Solomon's immense wealth did not bring him fulfillment, highlighting that true contentment comes from God, not from material riches. Jesus taught us to seek first the kingdom of God and His righteousness, and all these things will be added to us (Matthew 6:33).

Responsible Financial Practices

To achieve financial responsibility and establish good credit, it's crucial to evaluate each purchase wisely. The Bible advises us to be trustworthy stewards: "Moreover, it is required of stewards that they be found trustworthy" (1 Corinthians 4:2). Before making a purchase, consider the following questions:

a) Is this purchase a true need or just a desire?

b) Do I have adequate funds to purchase this without using credit?

c) Have I compared the cost of competing products?

d) Have I prayed about this purchase?

e) Have I been patient in waiting on God's provision?

f) Do I have God's peace regarding this purchase?

g) Does this purchase conform to the purpose God has for me?

Gratitude is a powerful antidote to impulse buying, as it creates a sense of abundance. "In everything give thanks: for this is the will of God in Christ Jesus concerning you" (1 Thessalonians 5:18).

Managing Money in Marriage

It is essential for married couples to communicate and agree on financial decisions. Amos 3:3 asks, "Can two walk together unless they are agreed?" This principle applies to financial decisions as well. Couples should discuss and agree on major purchases to ensure they are aligned and working towards common financial goals.

Biblical Principles for Financial Management

An individual can achieve financial freedom by adhering to five biblical principles:

a) The Law of Contentment: "But godliness with contentment is great gain" (1 Timothy 6:6).

b) The Law of Self-Control: "Like a city whose walls are broken through is a person who lacks self-control" (Proverbs 25:28).

c) The Law of Stewardship: "The earth is the Lord's, and everything in it" (Psalm 24:1).

d) The Law of Giving: "Each of you should give what you have decided in your heart to give, not reluctantly or under compulsion, for God loves a cheerful giver" (2 Corinthians 9:7).

e) The Law of Petition: "Ask, and it will be given to you; seek, and you will find; knock, and it will be opened to you" (Matthew 7:7).

Steps to Financial Freedom

To cancel debt and achieve financial freedom, consider the following steps (Proverbs 6:5):

a) Identify your debt situation.

b) Consider your lifestyle.

c) Establish financial goals.

d) Take action with your finances.

Praying for wisdom and trusting in God's provision is crucial. "If any of you lacks wisdom, you should ask God, who gives generously to all without finding fault, and it will be given to you" (James 1:5).

Conclusion

The Bible has predetermined your purpose as well as your money's purpose—it's all for the glory of God. By following biblical principles, practicing gratitude, and seeking God's wisdom, you can achieve financial freedom and live a life that honors Him. "So whether you eat or drink or whatever you do, do it all for the glory of God" (1 Corinthians 10:31).

CHAPTER 20

Forgiveness: The Freedom of Letting Go

"Bear with each other and forgive whatever grievances you may have against one another. Forgive as the Lord forgave you." (Colossians 3:13) Understanding Forgiveness

Forgiveness refers to the act of letting go of feelings of anger, resentment, or bitterness towards someone who has wronged or hurt you. It involves a willingness to release negative emotions and thoughts and to move forward with an attitude of understanding, compassion, and acceptance. The Bible teaches us the power of forgiveness: "Be kind and compassionate to one another, forgiving each other, just as in Christ God forgave you" (Ephesians 4:32).

The Power of Forgiveness

Forgiveness is a powerful tool that can help individuals heal emotional wounds, improve relationships, and reduce stress and anxiety. It can also contribute to improved mental and physical health by reducing negative emotions and improving overall well-being. Jesus emphasized the importance of forgiveness in the Lord's Prayer, "And forgive us our debts, as we also have forgiven our debtors" (Matthew 6:12).

What Forgiveness Is Not

Forgiveness does not mean forgetting the wrongdoing or excusing the offender's behavior. It is about choosing to release negative feelings and moving on from the situation. Forgiveness can be a difficult process and may require time and effort to achieve, but it can lead to greater peace, happiness, and emotional freedom. "Forgive as the Lord forgave you" (Colossians 3:13) reminds us that our forgiveness should reflect the forgiveness we have received from God.

The Benefits of Forgiveness

Forgiveness is not only beneficial for the person being forgiven but also for the person who forgives. It can help to reduce feelings of anger and resentment, improve relationships, and promote personal growth and development. "Blessed are the merciful, for they will be shown mercy" (Matthew 5:7).

The Personal Choice of Forgiveness

Ultimately, forgiveness is a personal choice that each individual must make for themselves. It requires courage, empathy, and compassion and can bring about powerful positive changes in both the individual and the world around them. "If you forgive other people when they sin against you, your heavenly Father will also forgive you" (Matthew 6:14).

The Nature of Forgiveness

According to Colossians 3:13, forgiveness is about:

a) Dismissing a debt: "And forgive us our debts, as we also have forgiven our debtors" (Matthew 6:12).

b) Releasing your demand: "Do not take revenge, my dear friends, but leave room for God's wrath" (Romans 12:19).

c) Letting go of resentment: "Get rid of all bitterness, rage and anger" (Ephesians 4:31).

d) Living joyfully and peacefully: "Peace I leave with you; my peace I give you" (John 14:27).

Misconceptions About Forgiveness

Misconceptions abound when the word forgiveness is mentioned. Some think that forgiveness is excusing sin and saying that what was wrong was right. But that is not true.

a) Forgiveness is not the same as reconciliation: "If it is possible, as far as it depends on you, live at peace with everyone" (Romans 12:18).

b) Forgiveness is not letting the guilty off the hook: "The Lord is a God who avenges" (Psalm 94:1).

c) Forgiveness is not being a weak martyr: "For the Spirit God gave us does not make us timid, but gives us power" (2 Timothy 1:7).

d) Forgiveness is not based on what is fair: "Forgive as the Lord forgave you" (Colossians 3:13).

God's Command on Forgiveness

a) God commands that we forgive each other: "Be kind and compassionate to one another, forgiving each other" (Ephesians 4:32).

b) God forgives us, so we must forgive others: "Forgive as the Lord forgave you" (Colossians 3:13).

c) Unforgiveness is sin: "If anyone, then, knows the good they ought to do and doesn't do it, it is sin for them" (James 4:17).

d) God desires a heart of mercy: "Blessed are the merciful" (Matthew 5:7).

e) Seek to live in peace: "If it is possible, as far as it depends on you, live at peace with everyone" (Romans 12:18).

f) Overcome evil with good: "Do not be overcome by evil, but overcome evil with good" (Romans 12:21).

g) Be ministers of reconciliation: "God... gave us the ministry of reconciliation" (2 Corinthians 5:18).

The Transformational Power of Forgiveness

To forgive those who sin against us requires the transformational power of God in our lives. There is something deep within fallen human nature that thirsts for revenge and urges retaliation. "But I tell you, love your enemies and pray for those who persecute you" (Matthew 5:44). Jesus gives us a heart willing to forgive and will work to that end.

The Gift of Forgiveness

When a person chooses to forgive, they give someone a gift—freedom from having to pay the penalty for offending them. This can be difficult, but it is also a gift to oneself—the gift of grudge-free living. "Do not seek revenge or bear a grudge against anyone among your people, but love your neighbor as yourself" (Leviticus 19:18).

The Stages of Forgiveness

The process of forgiveness involves several stages:

a) Face the offense: Acknowledge the hurt and pain it caused.

b) Feel the offense: Allow yourself to feel the emotions associated with the offense.

c) Forgive the offender: Release the offense and the offender.

d) Find oneness when appropriate: Rebuild the relationship if it is safe and healthy to do so.

Genuine Forgiveness and Healing

Genuine forgiveness draws individuals to the heart of God and facilitates healing. "The Lord is close to the brokenhearted and saves those who are crushed in spirit" (Psalm 34:18). It is important to process the painfully before healing can occur. "You desired faithfulness even in the womb; you taught me wisdom in that secret place" (Psalm 51:6).

Forgiveness and Personal Responsibility

Forgiveness is not about fairness. God knows how to deal with each person fairly—and He will in His own time. "Do not take revenge, my dear friends, but leave room for God's wrath" (Romans 12:19). Individuals cannot control others' actions but can control their response. "Then Peter came to Jesus and asked, 'Lord, how many times shall I forgive my brother or sister who sins against me? Up to seven times?' Jesus answered, 'I tell you, not seven times, but seventy-seven times'" (Matthew 18:21-22).

Moving Forward After Forgiveness

After forgiving someone, it is important to learn from the experience and move forward. "Forgetting what is behind and straining toward what is ahead" (Philippians 3:13). We should not allow a root of bitterness to spring up in our hearts. "See to it that no one falls short of the grace of God and that no bitter root grows up to cause trouble and defile many" (Hebrews 12:15).

Conditions for Reconciliation

Reconciliation depends on both parties' commitment to honesty and the following factors:

a) Has the offender taken responsibility for the wrong? "Whoever conceals their sins does not prosper, but the one who confesses and renounces them finds mercy" (Proverbs 28:13).

b) Is the offender being truthful? "The integrity of the upright guides them, but the unfaithful are destroyed by their duplicity" (Proverbs 11:3).

c) Does the offender show godly sorrow? "Godly sorrow brings repentance that leads to salvation and leaves no regret" (2 Corinthians 7:10-11).

When Reconciliation May Not Be Wise

While forgiveness is encouraged, reconciliation may not always be wise, especially in cases of severe harm like rape, adultery, or uncontrolled anger. Jesus empowers us to forgive, but He also gives us wisdom to protect ourselves and seek healthy boundaries.

Forgiveness is a divine command and a personal choice that brings freedom and healing. Jesus empowers us to forgive, reminding us that we have been forgiven much. "Forgive as the Lord forgave you"

(Colossians 3:13). Embracing forgiveness leads to a life of peace, joy, and a deeper relationship with God.

CHAPTER 21

Grief Recovery: Living at Peace with Loss

"Though he brings grief, he will show compassion, so great is His unfailing love. For he does not willingly bring affliction or grief to His children." (Lamentations 3:32-33)

The verse from Lamentations 3:32-33 highlights God's compassionate and loving nature toward His children. Even though there may be times of grief and affliction, God's love is unfailing, and He does not willfully bring harm or pain to His people. This verse assures us that God's compassion and love can bring about growth, maturity, and ultimately, greater joy and fulfillment in our lives, even through suffering and trials. "And we know that in all things God works for the good of those who love him" (Romans 8:28).

Understanding Grief

Grief is a heart response to hurt, a painful emotion of sorrow caused by the loss or impending loss of someone or something deeply meaningful. Bereavement specifically refers to the process of recovering from the death of a loved one. Grief, however, is a reaction to any form of loss and encompasses a range of feelings from deep sadness to anger. The process of adapting to significant loss can vary dramatically depending on one's background, beliefs, and relationship to what or who was lost. "The Lord is close to the brokenhearted and saves those who are crushed in spirit" (Psalm 34:18).

Jesus and Grief

God understands our anguish. Isaiah 53:3 describes Jesus as a "Man of sorrows, acquainted with grief." Jesus knew sorrow and grief intimately. This was not self-pity but a profound sorrow for others and the fallen condition of humanity. "He was despised and rejected by mankind, a man of suffering, and familiar with pain" (Isaiah 53:3).

The Purpose of Grief

The pain of grief is always purposeful. When grief accomplishes its work, it carves out a deep well within us that God Himself will fill with joy, peace, and contentment. "Blessed are those who mourn, for they will be comforted" (Matthew 5:4).

Stages of Grief

While stages of grief do exist, they may be experienced with varying degrees of intensity. Some stages may be missed, and others may be repeated. It is important for individuals experiencing grief to give themselves permission to unpredictably experience these stages and trust God to bring new life again. "He heals the brokenhearted and binds up their wounds" (Psalm 147:3).

The Three Stages of Healthy Grieving

Grief is so powerful that people often look for ways to avoid it rather than experience it. However, the best approach is to work through the stages of grief and express one's feelings. The three stages of healthy grieving are:

a) Crisis Stage: Anxiety, fear, confusion, denial, disturbing dreams, and uncontrollable crying. "Even though I walk through the darkest valley, I will fear no evil, for you are with me" (Psalm 23:4).

b) Crucible Stage: Anger, resentment, anguish, bargaining with God, depression, loneliness, self-pity, and guilt or false guilt. "Cast all your anxiety on him because he cares for you" (1 Peter 5:7).

c) Contentment Stage: Greater compassion toward others, greater acceptance, humility, and a greater dependence on the Lord. "The peace of God, which transcends all understanding, will guard your hearts and your minds in Christ Jesus" (Philippians 4:7).

Unhealthy Grief

The two types of unhealthy grief are:

a) Chronic Grief: Prolonged grief that persists and overwhelms. "Come to me, all you who are weary and burdened, and I will give you rest" (Matthew 11:28).

b) Repressed Grief: The suppression or denial of grief, which can lead to physical symptoms and long-term psychological problems. "When I kept silent, my bones wasted away through my groaning all day long" (Psalm 32:3).

Steps to Recovery

The path to recovery requires ministering to an individual's body, soul, and spirit to diminish painful emotions and assist them in finding their way out of despondency. "May the God of hope fill you with all joy and peace as you trust in him" (Romans 15:13).

Emotional Guidelines for Healthy Grieving

Healthy grieving involves several emotional guidelines:

a) Cultivate a Strong Support System: "As iron sharpens iron, so one person sharpens another" (Proverbs 27:17).

b) Cultivate the Freedom to Cry: "Those who sow with tears will reap with songs of joy" (Psalm 126:5).

c) Cultivate a Plan for Socializing: "Not giving up meeting together, as some are in the habit of doing, but encouraging one another" (Hebrews 10:25).

d) Cultivate a Trustworthy Confidante: "Two are better than one because they have a good return for their labor" (Ecclesiastes 4:9-10).

e) Cultivate the Release of Resentment: "Be kind and compassionate to one another, forgiving each other" (Ephesians 4:32).

Physical Guidelines for Healthy Grieving

Grieving also involves physical care:

a) Get Sufficient Rest: "My presence will go with you, and I will give you rest" (Exodus 33:14).

b) Stay Hydrated and Eat Nutritious Food: "Get up and eat, for the journey is too much for you" (1 Kings 19:7-8).

c) Engage in Regular Exercise: "For physical training is of some value" (1 Timothy 4:8).

d) Spend Time in the Sunshine: "Light is sweet, and it pleases the eyes to see the sun" (Ecclesiastes 11:7).

Spiritual Guidelines for Healthy Grieving

Spiritual care is essential for healthy grieving:

a) Develop a Purposeful Prayer Life: "I gave an account of my ways and you answered me; teach me your decrees" (Psalm 119:26).

b) Maintain a Positive Perspective: "Whatever is true, whatever is noble, whatever is right, whatever is pure, whatever is lovely, whatever is admirable—if anything is excellent or praiseworthy—think about such things" (Philippians 4:8).

c) Seek Peace about the Past: "If we confess our sins, he is faithful and just and will forgive us our sins" (1 John 1:9).

d) Memorize Scripture: "All Scripture is God-breathed and is useful for teaching, rebuking, correcting and training in righteousness" (2 Timothy 3:16-17).

e) Yearn for Eternity: "So we fix our eyes not on what is seen, but on what is unseen since what is seen is temporary, but what is unseen is eternal" (2 Corinthians 4:18).

Encouraging the Grieving Individual

A biblical counselor can help those who are grieving by extending a compassionate hand, lending a listening ear, and encouraging a broken heart. "A word fitly spoken is like apples of gold in pictures of silver" (Proverbs 25:11).

Practical Steps to Support Grieving Individuals

a) Acknowledge Their Loss Immediately: Show empathy and understanding. "Rejoice with those who rejoice; mourn with those who mourn" (Romans 12:15).

b) Accept All Emotional Responses without Judgment: Be patient and understanding. "Bear one another's burdens, and so fulfill the law of Christ" (Galatians 6:2).

c) Offer Physical Affection: "Greet one another with a holy kiss" (2 Corinthians 13:12).

d) Expect Tears and Emotional Extremes: Be prepared for varied emotional responses. "Jesus wept" (John 11:35).

e) Find Practical Ways to Help: Offer specific assistance. "Little children, let us not love in word or talk but in deed and in truth" (1 John 3:18).

f) Encourage Them to Talk About Their Loss: Provide a listening ear. "The heartfelt counsel of a friend is as sweet as perfume and incense" (Proverbs 27:9 NLT).

By following these guidelines, we can help those who are grieving find comfort, peace, and the strength to move forward. "Therefore encourage one another and build each other up" (1 Thessalonians 5:11).

C H A P T E R 2 2

The Guilt: Getting Rid of Guilt for Good

"Bear with each other and forgive whatever grievances you may have against one another. Forgive as the Lord forgave you." (Colossians 3:13)

Guilt is a feeling of responsibility or remorse for a perceived offense or wrongdoing, whether real or imagined. It is often associated with feelings of shame or regret and can result from actions taken or not taken, or from violating one's own values or beliefs. Guilt can be a normal response to certain situations, such as when we have hurt someone or acted in a way that is inconsistent with our values. However, when guilt becomes overwhelming or interferes with daily life, it may be helpful to seek support from a therapist or mental health professional.

God's Use of Guilt

God always uses guilt to convict, correct, and conform an individual's character. "Godly sorrow brings repentance that leads to salvation and leaves no regret, but worldly sorrow brings death" (2 Corinthians 7:10). Paul made the Corinthian Christians feel bad about their sins, but he did it in a godly way. He used the truth, not lies or exaggeration. He was honest, not using hidden agendas and manipulation. He simply told the truth in love.

The Reality of Guilt

From the earliest childhood, no one has escaped guilt. The Old Testament word "asham" has many derivatives. True guilt refers to the fact of being at fault, deserving punishment, and requiring a sacrificial offering. True guilt is the result of sin for which a penalty must be paid so that fellowship with God can be restored. "For all have sinned and fall short of the glory of God" (Romans 3:23).

Defining False Guilt

False guilt keeps a person in bondage through shame, fear, and anger, which come from the 'accuser of the brethren', Satan. False guilt arises when an individual blames themselves, even though they may have committed no wrong, or even though they have confessed and turned from their sin. False guilt is based on self-condemning feelings that an individual has not lived up to their own expectations or the expectations of others, and this type of guilt is not resolved by confession. "There is now no condemnation for those who are in Christ Jesus" (Romans 8:1).

The Burden of False Guilt

False guilt results in an individual being consumed by feelings. It creates spiritual and psychological cataracts, stopping us from seeing our relationships with God, others, and ourselves clearly. Through false guilt:

- We bear false witness against ourselves.
- We judge ourselves inaccurately and too harshly.

- False guilt puts heavy burdens upon our backs, burdens we were never intended to shoulder.

- False guilt is self-abuse.

- People who suffer from false guilt nearly always have difficulty being truthful about how they think, feel, and act.

The Purpose of True Guilt

True guilt results in repentance. Scripture is clear that all humanity is guilty before a holy God. Romans 3 teaches us that there is no person who is righteous and that in the face of a perfect law, all mouths are shut, and the whole world lies under judgment. "If we confess our sins, he is faithful and just and will forgive us our sins and purify us from all unrighteousness" (1 John 1:9). True guilt results in godly sorrow over sin, leading to acceptance of God's forgiveness and positive words of thankfulness.

Distinguishing True and False Guilt

When a person experiences true guilt, they will understand the appropriateness of the finished work of Christ at Calvary and that only Christ can meet all their needs. False guilt is manifested in an attitude of self-pity and is characterized by a focus on self and the need to perform many personal good works. "For it is by grace you have been saved, through faith—and this is not from yourselves, it is the gift of God" (Ephesians 2:8).

Satan's Accusations

The Bible says that Satan loves to disguise himself by masquerading as a spokesman for God. Brutally accusing and condemning those with a sensitive conscience, he uses undeserved guilt as his most powerful weapon. Satan will accuse us of:

- Sins we have committed but properly confessed.

- Sins and hurts for which we are not responsible.

- Issues and actions that are not morally wrong and therefore do not need to be confessed.

Learning to Discern

A Christian needs to learn to discern the lies of Satan to avoid spiritual discouragement. We need to filter our thoughts through scriptural truth. For instance, send troubling, guilt-ridden thoughts through the "filter" of Philippians 4:8: "Finally brothers, whatever is true, whatever is noble, whatever is right, whatever is pure, whatever is lovely, whatever is admirable—think about these things."

God's Conviction vs. Satan's Condemnation

We must learn to differentiate the lies of Satan through his condemnation and God's conviction. Satan uses unreasonable 'shoulds' to manipulate us, such as:

- Never display anger or disappointment.

- Be able to get over your loss and pain quickly.

- Never cry or show weakness.

- Be the perfect mate, parent, friend, employee, or church member.

Steps to Transformation and Freedom

The eight steps toward the road to transformation and maturity, which can help an individual find freedom and forgiveness from guilt, are represented by the acronym F-O-R-G-I-V-E-N:

a) Find the source of your guilt.

b) Own responsibility for your sin.

c) Realize God means what He says.

d) Give up dwelling on the past. False guilt can result in depression and spiritual paralysis. The cure for false guilt is the gospel.

e) Invest time in renewing your mind.

f) Verify truth when Satan accuses. Sometimes false guilt can be planted so deeply in our hearts that we need more than one person to minister truth to us. "A matter must be established by the testimony of two or three witnesses" (Deuteronomy 19:15).

g) Exchange your life for the life of Christ.

h) Notice God brings your feeling in line with the fact when you obey Him.

Praying Over Guilt

In assisting an individual to pray over their feelings of guilt, the counselor might suggest praying for:

a) Discernment to know when I am feeling false guilt instead of true guilt.

b) The Holy Spirit to convict when I am heading in the wrong way so that I can get on the right path.

c) Sensitivity to the convicting touch of the Holy Spirit's hand.

The Self-Imposed Prison of Guilt

Guilt can covertly construct a self-imposed prison in an individual's life. This prison limits opportunities due to beliefs, fears, or behaviors. Breaking free from a self-imposed prison requires self-awareness, a willingness to challenge one's beliefs and behaviors, and seeking help if needed. "It is for freedom that Christ has set us free. Stand firm, then, and do not let yourselves be burdened again by a yoke of slavery" (Galatians 5:1).

Overcoming False Guilt

If you counsel someone suffering from false guilt, encourage them to:

- Focus on the grace of God. "But where sin increased, grace increased all the more" (Romans 5:20).

- Meditate on Romans 8:1: "There is therefore now no condemnation for those who are in Christ Jesus."

- Preach the gospel to yourself every day, spending time in passages such as Romans 3:19-26, Psalm 103:8-13, Romans 4:7-8, Ephesians 1:3-11, and Romans 5:6-11.

- Meditate on the cross and all it means to you. Never think of your sin without also remembering the cross and the grace of God displayed in it.

Habits: Success in Self-Control

"Clothe yourself with the Lord Jesus Christ, And do not think about how to gratify the desires of the sinful nature." (Romans 13:14)

Success in self-control refers to the ability to manage one's impulses, emotions, and actions in order to achieve long-term goals and live in alignment with one's values. It involves making conscious choices and resisting short-term gratification in favor of long-term benefits. Proverbs 25:28 reminds us, "Like a city whose walls are broken through is a person who lacks self-control."

Self-control is a crucial element in achieving success in various areas of life, including personal growth, relationships, career, and health. For example, maintaining a healthy diet and exercise routine requires self-control in resisting unhealthy foods and prioritizing physical activity. Similarly, building strong relationships requires self-control in managing one's emotions and behaviors during conflicts.

Galatians 5:22-23 tells us that self-control is a fruit of the Spirit, highlighting its importance in a godly life.

Tips for Achieving Success in Self-Control

1. Set Clear Goals: Having clear, specific goals helps to clarify priorities and motivate action towards achieving them. Proverbs 21:5 says, "The plans of the diligent lead surely to abundance, but everyone who is hasty comes only to poverty."

2. Identify Triggers: Recognizing situations or emotions that trigger impulsive behavior can help to proactively manage them. James 1:14-15 warns that each person is tempted when they are dragged away by their own evil desire and enticed.

3. Practice Mindfulness: Mindfulness techniques such as meditation or deep breathing can help to increase self-awareness and manage stress levels, reducing the likelihood of impulsive behavior. Psalm 46:10 encourages us to "Be still, and know that I am God."

4. Develop Healthy Habits: Creating healthy habits such as regular exercise or a consistent sleep schedule can help to strengthen self-control and reduce the likelihood of impulsive behavior. 1 Corinthians 6:19-20 reminds us that our bodies are temples of the Holy Spirit and should be treated with respect.

5. Seek Support: Seeking support from friends, family, or professionals can provide accountability and help to manage stress or difficult emotions that may challenge self-control. Ecclesiastes 4:9-10 highlights the strength of companionship and mutual support.

The Nature of Self-Control

Self-control ("temperance" in the KJV) is the ability to control oneself. It involves moderation, constraint, and the ability to say "no" to our baser desires and fleshly lusts. Titus 2:11-12 teaches us that the grace of God instructs us to live self-controlled, upright, and godly lives.

Characteristics of Habits

- Regularity: Habits occur with regularity.

- Automaticity: Habits happen without thinking.

- Reflection of Inner Morals: Habits reflect inner morals.

- Growth: Habits tend to grow stronger and more ingrained over time.

- Persistence: Habits persist and become hard to change.

- Pleasure: Habits provide some degree of pleasure.

Signs of Unhealthy Habits

An unhealthy habit can control and have mastery over an individual. Signs include harm to health and finances, defensive behavior when confronted, and thoughts and time consumed by the habit. Romans 6:16 warns us that we become slaves to whatever we obey.

God's Power Over Sin

One proof of God's working in our lives is the ability to control our thoughts, words, and actions. Without the power of the Holy Spirit, we are incapable of knowing and choosing how best to meet our needs. Psalm 139:23-24 offers a prayer for divine help: "Search me, God, and know my heart; test me and know my anxious thoughts. See if there is any offensive way in me, and lead me in the way everlasting."

Factors Fueling Negative Habits

1. Misguided Choices

2. Misplaced Dependencies

3. Misaligned Beliefs

These factors highlight the ease with which our human appetites can lead to sinful excesses if not controlled. 1 Corinthians 9:25 emphasizes the importance of self-discipline: "Everyone who competes in the games goes into strict training. They do it to get a crown that will not last, but we do it to get a crown that will last forever."

A Godly Approach to Breaking Negative Habits

Breaking negative habits involves depending on the Lord to meet all our needs for love, significance, and security. Colossians 1:27 reminds us of Christ in us, the hope of glory. This assures us that we are never alone during times of temptation. Philippians 4:13 strengthens us with the promise that we can do all things through Christ who strengthens us.

Steps to Self-Control

1. Commit to God: Commit to following God's ways.

2. Separate from Sin: Avoid situations that tempt you.

3. Set New Goals: Focus on godly objectives.

4. Stand on the Truth: Rely on God's Word.

5. Substitute God's Thoughts: Replace negative thoughts with Scripture.

6. Surrender Your Will: Yield to the Holy Spirit.

7. Stay on Track: Persevere in faith and action.

Replacing Bad Habits with Good Ones

Believers need self-control because the outside world and internal forces still attack (Romans 7:21-25). Like a vulnerable city, we must have defenses, such as avoiding close relationships with sinners, meeting with other believers, and meditating on the Word of God.

Clothed in Christ's Character

We transform our character by taking off the tattered rags of sin and replacing them with Christ's apparel. Steps include:

1. Put on the Habit of Faith.

2. Put on the Habit of Goodness.

3. Put on the Habit of Knowledge.

4. Put on the Habit of Perseverance.

5. Put on the Habit of Godliness.

6. Put on the Habit of Brotherly Kindness.

7. Put on the Habit of Love.

2 Peter 1:5-7 encourages us to make every effort to add to our faith goodness, knowledge, self-control, perseverance, godliness, mutual affection, and love.

Changing Childhood Habits

Many habits stem from childhood experiences. It is possible to change habits reflecting a negative childhood mindset by choosing to sow good habits. Ephesians 4:22-24 advises us to "put off your old self" and "put on the new self, created to be like God in true righteousness and holiness."

Sowing Seeds of Good Habits

If an individual has accepted Christ as their Savior, they can choose to plant, cultivate, and harvest good habits that are desirable and pleasing to God. We are called to sow seeds of moral sensitivities, accountability, gratefulness, forgiveness, selflessness, and communion with God.

The Work of the Holy Spirit

Self-control is a work of the Holy Spirit, not the individual. Galatians 5:22-23 lists the fruit of the Spirit, emphasizing that it is the Holy Spirit who produces self-control in us. Paul said, "God did not give us a Spirit of timidity, but a Spirit of power, of love and of self-discipline" (2 Timothy 1:7). Indeed, Christians are controlled not by the sinful nature, but by the Holy Spirit (Romans 8:9), who helps us in our weakness (v.26), making us able to say "no" to sin.

By embracing these biblical principles and relying on the Holy Spirit, individuals can develop the self-control needed to live a life that honors God and achieves their long-term goals.

C H A P T E R   2 4

Homosexuality: A Case of Mistaken Identity

"Do not lie with a man as one lies with a woman; that is detestable." (Leviticus 18:22)

True Identity in God's Creation

Same-sex attraction does not reflect an individual's true identity as created by God. Sexuality is sacred, as God created male and female (Genesis 1:27), each with unique physiological and psychological traits designed to complement one another. Gender is far more than physical attributes; it forms the foundation of our identity. The trend of allowing children to choose their gender undermines God's intentional design and is inconsistent with biblical truth.

The Need for God's Truth

Same-sex attraction can result in a mistaken identity, creating a desperate need for truth — God's truth (John 8:32). The Bible teaches that God does not create people with homosexual desires.

Homosexuality arises from sin (Romans 1:24-27) and is ultimately a choice. While some may have a greater susceptibility to homosexual tendencies, just as others might have tendencies towards anger or violence, these inclinations do not justify sinful behavior. Just as giving in to anger is not excused, neither is yielding to homosexual desires.

Knowing God's Truth

Jesus said in John 8:32, "You will know the truth, and the truth will set you free." Discerning what is right in God's sight requires knowing the truths of Scripture and understanding the character of God:

- "God is Love" (1 John 4:16)
- "God is Holy" (Psalm 99:9)
- "Be Holy because I, the Lord your God, am Holy" (Leviticus 19:2)

Biblical Condemnation of Homosexuality

Several Bible passages verify that homosexuality is a sin:
- Leviticus 18:22
- Genesis 19:4-7
- Leviticus 20:13

The Bible consistently condemns homosexual activity (Genesis 19:1-13; Leviticus 18:22; 20:13; Romans 1:26-27; 1 Corinthians 6:9). Romans 1:26-27 specifically teaches that homosexuality results from denying and disobeying God. Continued sin and unbelief lead to God "giving them over" to more wicked and depraved acts to highlight the futility of life apart from Him. 1 Corinthians 6:9 warns that homosexual offenders will not inherit the kingdom of God.

Same-Sex Attraction and Sin

While same-sex attraction is abnormal and unnatural, it is a result of humanity's sinfulness (Romans 3:23). These attractions can stem from various influences, but acting on them is sinful. There is no scientific evidence for a 'homosexual gene'; the primary influences are environmental factors and personal responses to those environments.

Risky Behavior

Homosexuality is associated with risky behaviors. Although homosexuals constitute approximately 2%-4% of the population, they have a significantly higher risk of contracting AIDS and other sexually transmitted diseases. Moreover, they face higher rates of various cancers, eating disorders, anxiety, psychiatric disorders, substance abuse, depression, and suicide. These statistics highlight the devastating impact of homosexuality on physical and mental health.

Christian Response to Homosexuality

Many homosexuals feel condemned by the church, often due to unloving attitudes from Christians. However, Christians are called to love everyone while declaring God's truth about sin. This is not condemnation but an offer of hope for forgiveness and transformation through Christ (Psalm 119:9-11).

Forgiveness and Transformation

The Bible does not rank homosexuality as a greater sin than others. All sin is offensive to God, and His forgiveness is available to everyone, including homosexuals (1 Corinthians 6:11; 2 Corinthians 5:17; Philippians 4:13). God provides the strength to overcome all sin, including homosexuality.

Scriptural Standards

The Bible consistently presents God's standards regarding homosexuality:

- Genesis 19:4-5, 7
- Leviticus 20:13
- Judges 19:22-23
- 1 Corinthians 6:9-10

Factors Leading to Homosexuality

Various factors can lead to homosexual relationships, including weak or absent fathers, lack of bonding with fathers, and mistreatment by significant males. Similarly, girls may turn to lesbian relationships due to weak or non-nurturing mothers, or abusive fathers.

Positive Steps Toward Recovery

Individuals caught in a homosexual lifestyle can find freedom and align with God's plan for their sexuality by:

1. Focusing on God's Love: "See what great love the Father has lavished on us" (1 John 3:1).

2. Owning Negative Emotions: Recognize and address past pain.

3. Refusing Irrational Emotions: Do not act on them.

4. Making Forgiveness a Priority: Forgive as the Lord forgave you (Colossians 3:13).

5. Identifying Triggers: Be aware of what leads to temptation.

6. Embracing True Identity: Understand oneself as a "Child of God" (Galatians 3:26).

New Life in Christ

Homosexual behavior, like any sin, separates us from God. However, surrendering to Jesus brings a new nature (2 Corinthians 5:17), freeing us from sin's power (Romans 6:1-7). While temptations persist, the Holy Spirit empowers believers to resist and overcome sin (Colossians 2:14; James 4:7). In Christ, old identities fall away, and we are transformed into His likeness (1 John 3:9-10).

By embracing these biblical principles and relying on God's power, individuals can find freedom from homosexuality and live in alignment with their true identity in Christ.

C H A P T E R   2 5

Hope Anchor for Your Soul

"Blessed are those whose help is the God of Jacob, whose hope is in the LORD their God." (Psalm 146:5, NIV)

"Those who listen to instruction will prosper; those who trust the LORD will be joyful." (Proverbs 16:20, NLT)

Understanding Hope in the Lord

Hope in the Lord is a positive and optimistic state of mind and spirit based on the belief that good things will happen because the Lord is on your side. It is the conviction that things will ultimately work out for the best, even if the current situation is difficult or uncertain. Isaiah 40:31 (KJV) reminds us, "But they that wait upon the LORD shall renew their strength; they shall mount up with wings as eagles; they shall run, and not be weary; and they shall walk, and not faint." This kind of hope motivates individuals to persevere through hardships, providing a sense of purpose and direction.

The Source of Hope

Hope can be grounded in various beliefs and sources, such as faith in God, trust in His promises, and the conviction that His Word is true. Psalm 62:5-7 says, "Find rest, O my soul, in God alone; my hope comes from him. He alone is my rock and my salvation; he is my fortress, I will not be shaken. My salvation and my honor depend on God; he is my mighty rock, my refuge." This hope is not wishful thinking or denial but acknowledges challenges while maintaining a belief that positive outcomes are possible.

Benefits of Hope

Hope has positive effects on mental and physical health. Research shows that individuals with a sense of hopefulness and optimism have better coping skills, higher resilience, and lower rates of depression and anxiety. Romans 15:13 (NIV) says, "May the God of hope fill you with all joy and peace as you trust in him, so that you may overflow with hope by the power of the Holy Spirit."

Biblical Definition of Hope

The popular understanding of hope is an optimistic wish, but Christian hope is based on God's unchanging Word and His assurance that His promises will be fulfilled. Romans 8:24-25 (NIV) states, "For in this hope we were saved. But hope that is seen is no hope at all. Who hopes for what they already have? But if we hope for what we do not yet have, we wait for it patiently." Hope is a firm assurance regarding things that are unclear and unknown (Hebrews 11:1, 7).

Anchored in God

When your hope is anchored in God, He teaches you His truth and leads you in the way you should go. Psalm 25:5 says, "Guide me in your truth and teach me, for you are God my Savior, and my hope is in you all day long." Placing one's hope in God brings comfort and confidence amid life's challenges.

Hope vs. Hopelessness

Hopelessness is characterized by absolute despair with no expectation of good, often leading to a desire to die. Hope, however, is an assured promise, while faith is acting on that promise. Hebrews 10:23 (NIV) encourages us, "Let us hold unswervingly to the hope we profess, for he who promised is faithful."

Qualities Christ Gives Through Hope

When individuals have put their faith in Christ, they can have hope and security in life's storms. Christ gives them qualities such as:

- Contentment (Philippians 4:11)

- Courage (Deuteronomy 31:6)

- Confidence (Hebrews 4:16)

- Cheerfulness (John 16:33)

- Comfort (2 Corinthians 1:3-4)

- Conviction (Romans 8:38-39)

- Christlikeness (Galatians 2:20)

Regaining Lost Hope

After losing hope, regaining it involves not focusing on the storm but on God's promises and His path for recovery. Jeremiah 29:11 (NIV) assures us, "For I know the plans I have for you," declares the LORD, "plans to prosper you and not to harm you, plans to give you hope and a future."

Cultivating Hope in Christ

Counselors can guide individuals to put their hope in Christ by:

- Looking at the situation accurately (Psalm 34:18)

- Aligning their thinking with what gives hope (Philippians 4:8)

- Learning what gives hope in the midst of the situation (Romans 8:28)

- Linger on the fact that God is faithful every day (Lamentations 3:22-23)

- Letting the Lord fulfill them completely (Psalm 37:4)

- Leaning on the truth to receive hope for the heart (Hebrews 6:19)

Overcoming Grief with Hope

To overcome grief with hope, individuals can:

- Realize they have a Savior who experienced severe grief (Isaiah 53:3)

- Remember that some grief and suffering are natural and must be endured (Ecclesiastes 3:1-4)

- Reach out to God in their sorrow (Psalm 34:17)

- Reflect on fond memories and allow themselves to grieve (Psalm 147:3)

- Reach out to a friend to share their pain (Galatians 6:2)

- Remain hopeful, knowing the feeling of deep grief will pass (Psalm 30:5)

- Reinforce their faith by giving hope to others (2 Corinthians 1:3-4)

Overcoming Bitterness with Hope

Counselors can assist individuals in overcoming bitterness by encouraging them to:

- Believe it is possible, with God's help, to get rid of all resentment (Ephesians 4:31-32)

- Know they are not helpless victims of others (Philippians 4:13)

- Take personal responsibility for their attitude of bitterness (Romans 12:18)

- Confess before God their harboring of anger (1 John 1:9)

- Search their hearts for past events or people that embitter them and release the desire for revenge (Romans 12:19)

- Understand that only a close relationship with Jesus can provide the love and confidence to let go (John 15:5)

- Cultivate a heart of forgiveness to experience God's total forgiveness (Matthew 6:14-15)

Benefits of Hope in Christ

Serving God brings benefits based on His promises, not because we earn them, but because of His grace. These benefits include:

- Generating faith and love in you (1 Corinthians 13:13)
- Causing you to live a pure life (1 John 3:3)
- Inspiring you to persevere with endurance (Hebrews 12:1-2)
- Uplifting your downcast soul (Psalm 42:11)
- Causing you to praise God (Psalm 71:14)
- Anchoring your soul (Hebrews 6:19)
- Giving you a reason to rejoice (Romans 12:12)
- Establishing your security and safety (Proverbs 14:26)
- Guaranteeing your eternal life (John 3:16)
- Being the Savior of all men (1 Timothy 4:10)

Who God is During Storms

In Christ, we have an anchor securing us through our storms. His holding power is unquestionable, and He holds us secure in His arms. Along with faith and love, hope is an enduring virtue of the Christian life (1 Corinthians 13:13), and love springs from hope (Colossians 1:4-5). Hope produces joy and peace in believers through the power of the Spirit (Romans 15:13). Paul attributes his apostolic calling to the hope of eternal glory (Titus 1:1-2). Hope in Christ's return motivates believers to purify themselves in this life (Titus 2:11-14, 1 John 3:3).

By embracing these biblical principles and relying on God's power, individuals can find true hope and live a fulfilling life anchored in the promises of God.

CHAPTER 26

Identity: Do You Know Who You Really Are?

"Therefore if anyone is in Christ, he is a new creation; the old has gone, the new has come." (2 Corinthians 5:17)

Identity Beyond Occupation

Often, an individual's identity is self-described through their occupation. This is common in our society and allows for potential further discussion, helping us learn more about someone we have just met. While understanding someone's profession provides insight into their life, it doesn't capture the essence of who they truly are.

Nationality and Struggles

Our nationality and struggles, such as identifying as "I am an alcoholic," further distinguish us from one another. When traveling abroad, we might say, "I'm an American." At home, we might identify by our family roles, like "I'm married and have two children," or by our cultural background, like "I'm Italian and I love to cook." Disabilities also often define how people identify themselves. Yet, few of us identify ourselves by our faith. However, the true essence of our identity is found in how we are known by God—our basic nature, character, and value system.

Claiming Your Identity in Christ

In claiming our identity in Christ, to walk in victory, we need to identify the lies we believe about ourselves and find a path to recovery, discovering who we really are in Christ. Our lifestyle or way of life is important to the Lord; the Bible mentions our "walk" 229 times. Our walk should reflect our identity in Christ, as described in Ephesians 4:1, which urges us to "live a life worthy of the calling you have received."

Lasting Change Through Christ

Lasting change occurs when we claim our identity in Christ, reject the lies we believe, and constantly rely on the truth of Scripture. This makes us mature in Him, where it's the Savior, not our sins, that characterizes us and our true identities. Romans 12:2 (NIV) urges us, "Do not conform to the pattern of this world, but be transformed by the renewing of your mind." In Christ, we are no longer slaves to sin (Romans 6:6), but reconciled to God (Romans 5:10). This new identity changes our relationships with God, family, friends, and co-workers, and alters our view of the world.

Lies and Truths About Our Identity

The seven lies we tell ourselves, contrasted with the seven truths from God's Word, help us reclaim our true identity:

1. Lie 1: I can't feel valuable unless I am loved and accepted by significant people in my life.

Truth: You have God-given value because you are unconditionally loved and accepted by God. (Ephesians 1:5-6)

2. Lie 2: I will never feel valuable because this is just the way I am. I cannot change.

Truth: You have God-given value because God has changed you on the inside and given you new characteristics. (2 Corinthians 5:17)

3. Lie 3: I can't feel I have value unless I live in the right neighborhood, drive the right car, and wear the right clothes.

Truth: You have God-given value because you have a new residence in God's kingdom and are clothed in Christ. (Galatians 3:27)

4. Lie 4: My life has no value since I have done so many things wrong- my life is ruined.

Truth: You have God-given value because you have been given a new life in Jesus Christ. (Romans 8:1)

5. Lie 5: My life has value as long as I can look good to others.

Truth: You have God-given value even though you have fallen in the past and may stumble in the future. He has given you a new image. (1 John 1:9)

6. Lie 6: My life has no value because I have failed and deserve to be punished.

Truth: You have God-given value based not on your past performance but on Christ, who lives in you and gives you freedom from condemnation. (Romans 8:1-2)

7. Lie 7: My life has no value if I do not succeed financially and leave a comfortable inheritance.

Truth: You have God-given value because you have been given a new inheritance that provides the only true and lasting significance and security possible. (1 Peter 1:3-4)

Value Through Christ's Ownership

Sometimes, an item's value increases because of who owned it. For instance, a car once owned by Elvis Presley is more valuable than the average car. Our value is based on who owns us and the price paid for us. The Bible says, "You were bought at a price. Therefore honor God with your bodies." (1 Corinthians 6:20). Christ paid the ultimate price for us on the Cross, proving our immense value to Him. We are not junk; we are incredibly valuable to God.

Embracing Our Identity in Christ

In summary, to truly know who you are, embrace your identity in Christ. Recognize the lies that distort your perception and replace them with the truths found in God's Word. By doing so, you will walk in the freedom and confidence that comes from knowing you are valued and loved by God. As Galatians 2:20 (NIV) states, "I have been crucified with Christ and I no longer live, but Christ lives in me. The life I now live in the body, I live by faith in the Son of God, who loved me and gave himself for me."

CHAPTER 27

Illness- Chronic and Terminal: God's Peace amid Pain

1 Peter 1:24 (NIV): "All men are like grass, and all their glory is like the flowers of the field; the grass withers and the flowers fall."

Understanding Suffering

a) Troubles are temporary, glory is eternal. (2 Corinthians 4:16-18):

Paul was well-acquainted with suffering. In 2 Corinthians 11:23-28, he recounts his hardships: stripes, prisons, beatings, stoning, shipwrecks, perils in various situations, weariness, toil, sleeplessness, hunger, thirst, fasting, cold, and nakedness. Despite these trials, Paul viewed them as temporary afflictions leading to eternal glory. He said, "For our light and momentary troubles are achieving for us an eternal glory that far outweighs them all" (2 Corinthians 4:17). This perspective is crucial for enduring suffering with hope.

b) Your physical body is designed to decay. (Genesis 3:19):

Genesis 2:7 reveals that God formed man from the dust of the ground. Yet, due to sin, aging, deterioration, and death are inevitable parts of our existence. From dust we came, and to dust we shall return (Genesis 3:19; Ecclesiastes 3:20). However, our resurrection bodies will be imperishable and free from sickness, decay, or death (1 Corinthians 15:42-44).

c) Afflictions are allowed by God to teach you. (Psalm 119:71):

Afflictions serve a divine purpose, shaping us and teaching us God's statutes. Psalm 119:71 states, "It was good for me to be afflicted so that I might learn your decrees."

d) Lives are conformed to the image of Christ through suffering. (Romans 8:28-29):

God uses all things, including suffering, to conform us to the image of His Son. Romans 8:28-29 reminds us that "in all things God works for the good of those who love him, who have been called according to his purpose."

Stages of Sorrow

a) Denial - avoiding painful reality: Denial is a defense mechanism to shield oneself from the initial shock of a terminal diagnosis.

b) Anger - opening up honest emotions: In this stage, individuals may feel anger towards others or even God. This anger is a natural response to the perceived unfairness of the situation. "Why, God, have You let this happen?" (Psalm 13:1).

c) Bargaining - attempting to change reality: Individuals might attempt to negotiate with God, seeking more time or miraculous healing. "Lord, if You let me live, I will..."

d) Depression - feeling despair over the situation: This stage involves profound sadness and despair, feeling the weight of the illness and its implications. "My soul is weary with sorrow; strengthen me according to your word" (Psalm 119:28).

e) Acceptance - gaining a positive outlook: Acceptance brings a sense of peace, understanding that while we may not control our circumstances, we can trust God's plan. "And the peace of God, which transcends all understanding, will guard your hearts and your minds in Christ Jesus" (Philippians 4:7).

Healing and God's Will

God's Healing Power: God can heal anyone at any time, in any way. However, not all receive physical healing. It's essential to seek God's will for emotional, psychological, and spiritual healing. Psalm 147:3 assures us, "He heals the brokenhearted and binds up their wounds."

Understanding Death:

a) Death is Designed: God has appointed a time for each person. "Just as people are destined to die once, and after that to face judgment" (Hebrews 9:27).

b) Death is a Doorway: Our last breath on earth will be our first in eternity with God. "For to me, to live is Christ and to die is gain" (Philippians 1:21).

c) Death is Divine: It is under God's sovereign control. "Precious in the sight of the Lord is the death of his faithful servants" (Psalm 116:15).

Heaven's Assurance

What is Heaven Like?

a) Revelation 7:16: Heaven is a place without hunger or thirst.

b) Revelation 21:4: Heaven is a place without crying or pain.

c) Revelation 21:27: Heaven is a place without impurity or evil.

Preparing for the End

Put Your House in Order (2 Kings 20:1): The best advice for someone who is terminally ill is to prepare their affairs to ease their family's burdens.

Steps to Ease Loved Ones' Burdens:

a) Preparing a legally binding will (Hebrews 9:17): A testament takes effect upon the testator's death.

b) Expressing your desires (Hebrews 11:22): Like Joseph, express your wishes clearly for after your passing.

c) Arranging your affairs (1 Chronicles 28:11, 19): Organize your belongings and responsibilities.

d) Leaving a legacy of love (2 Timothy 1:3-4): Ensure your love and faith are remembered.

e) Trusting in God (Proverbs 19:21; Isaiah 55:8; Romans 8:28; 2 Timothy 2:13): Lean on His promises.

f) Yielding your heart (Matthew 26:39; Philippians 2:8; Ephesians 3:16; Philippians 4:13; 1 Corinthians 2:9): Surrender fully to God's will.

Leading Someone to Christ

When leading someone who is terminally ill to Christ, emphasize Jesus' love and the hope of eternal life through Him. Share the gospel, affirming that Jesus died for their sins and desires to spend eternity with them. Pray with them, guiding them to accept Christ as their Savior. This decision transforms death into a doorway to eternal life with God.

Any illness can be a burden and also a blessing: When difficulty draws us closer to the Lord, the gift tag reads, "Grace from God included." "But he said to me, 'My grace is sufficient for you, for my power is made perfect in weakness.' Therefore I will boast all the more gladly about my weaknesses, so that Christ's power may rest on me" (2 Corinthians 12:9).

CHAPTER 28

Lying: Stopping Truth Decay

Hebrews 4:13 (NIV): "Nothing in all creation is hidden from God's sight. Everything is uncovered and laid bare before the eyes of him to whom we must give account."

Understanding Lying

Lying is intentionally making a false statement or deliberately deceiving someone by presenting a false impression. It involves saying something that is not true or withholding information to mislead or deceive others. Proverbs 12:22 states, "The Lord detests lying lips, but he delights in people who are trustworthy."

Lying can take many forms, ranging from simple, everyday lies to more serious and damaging forms of deception. Examples of lying include telling a falsehood to avoid getting in trouble, making up a story to impress others, or concealing information to gain an advantage over others. This is why Ephesians 4:25 emphasizes, "Therefore each of you must put off falsehood and speak truthfully to your neighbor, for we are all members of one body."

While lying is generally considered to be a negative behavior, there are some instances where it may be seen as justified or even necessary, such as when it is used to protect someone from harm or to prevent a greater harm from occurring. However, God's Word is clear: "Do not lie to each other, since you have taken off your old self with its practices" (Colossians 3:9).

The Consequences of Lying

Lying can have severe negative consequences. It can erode trust in relationships, damage reputations, and harm personal and professional relationships. In some cases, lying may also be illegal, such as when it involves fraud or perjury in a court of law. Proverbs 19:5 warns, "A false witness will not go unpunished, and whoever pours out lies will not go free."

Overall, while lying may sometimes be seen as a means to an end, it is generally viewed as a negative behavior that can have serious consequences. Being truthful and honest fosters trust and mutual respect in relationships and promotes a more positive and ethical society. "The integrity of the upright guides them, but the unfaithful are destroyed by their duplicity" (Proverbs 11:3).

Types of Untruths

There are no lies that are harmless. All untruths can cause harm. Identifying the types of untruths meant to deceive is essential:

- White Lies: These are untrue statements considered unimportant or told to avoid hurting someone's feelings. However, "Encourage one another daily...so that none of you may be hardened by sin's deceitfulness" (Hebrews 3:13). God's condemnation of lying in Proverbs 6:16–19 contains no exception clause.

- Deception: Intentionally giving a false impression through a statement or omission. "Everyone lies to their neighbor; they flatter with their lips but harbor deception in their hearts" (Psalm 12:2).

- Duplicity: A form of deception where a person gives two different and opposing impressions. Proverbs 11:3 states, "The integrity of the upright guides them, but the unfaithful are destroyed by their duplicity."

- Half-Truths: Partially true statements made with the intent to deceive. Genesis 12:13 recounts Abraham's deception about Sarah being his sister.

- Perjury: A false testimony given under oath. Deuteronomy 19:16-20 discusses the seriousness of giving false testimony.

Despite some instances in the Bible where lying seemed to produce favorable outcomes (e.g., the Hebrew midwives in Exodus 1:15-21 or Rahab in Joshua 2:5), the Bible never praises the lies themselves or condones lying. The outcomes were part of God's mercy and plan, not an endorsement of the deceit.

Causes of Lying

Liars often lie to meet their needs or to avoid looking bad. Two primary causes for lying are:

1. Feeling Insignificant: Lying to appear more important.

2. Feeling Insecure: Lying to avoid looking bad, stupid, or inadequate.

Philippians 4:19 assures us, "And my God will meet all your needs according to the riches of his glory in Christ Jesus." Understanding this truth helps us resist the temptation to lie.

Encouraging Truth-Telling

Encouraging truth-telling in difficult situations involves several principles:

1. Know that you cannot please everyone. Galatians 1:10 says, "Am I now trying to win the approval of human beings, or of God? Or am I trying to please people? If I were still trying to please people, I would not be a servant of Christ."

2. Know that you are not responsible for everyone's feelings. Proverbs 9:7-9 teaches, "Whoever corrects a mocker invites insults; whoever rebukes the wicked incurs abuse. Do not rebuke mockers or they will hate you; rebuke the wise and they will love you."

3. Know that you can speak the truth in a loving way. Ephesians 4:15 instructs us to "speak the truth in love."

4. Know that you are not perfect. Isaiah 53:6 reminds us, "We all, like sheep, have gone astray, each of us has turned to our own way; and the Lord has laid on him the iniquity of us all."

5. Know that you are accountable to God. Romans 14:12 states, "So then, each of us will give an account of ourselves to God."

Lies propagate themselves and complicate relationships, making further lying even more likely. Telling the truth is precious to God (Proverbs 12:22) and demonstrates the fear of the Lord.

Steps to Honesty

Six steps on the path to recovery, exchanging half-truths for honesty, are essential for deliverance from deceit:

1. Determine to be honest with God and admit your failures.

2. Discern your areas of personal temptation and think before you answer.

3. Decide to reflect Christ, who lives in you. Colossians 1:27 says, "Christ in you, the hope of glory."

4. Depend on Christ's strength to enable change. Philippians 4:13 assures, "I can do all this through him who gives me strength."

5. Delight in speaking the truth, which is more rewarding than lies. Proverbs 12:19 states, "Truthful lips endure forever, but a lying tongue lasts only a moment."

6. Discover God's consequences for lying and His hatred for deceit. Proverbs 6:16-19 lists lying as one of the things God hates.

Being truthful is not a suggestion but a command (Psalm 15:2; Zechariah 8:16; Ephesians 4:25). It honors the Lord, the "God of truth" (Psalm 31:5), and stands against Satan, the "father of lies" (John 8:44).

CHAPTER 29

Manipulation: Severing the String of Control

Matthew 7:15 (NIV): "Beware of false prophets, who come to you in sheep's clothing but inwardly are ravenous wolves."

Understanding Manipulation

Manipulation is the act of controlling or influencing someone in a way that is often deceptive or unfair, typically for personal gain or advantage. It involves using various tactics to get someone to do something they may not otherwise choose to do. This behavior is condemned in Proverbs 26:24, which says, "A malicious man disguises himself with his lips, but in his heart he harbors deceit."

Manipulation can take many forms, such as guilt-tripping, emotional blackmail, gaslighting, flattery, or playing on someone's fears or insecurities. It can occur in personal relationships, professional settings, or social interactions. The effects of manipulation can be damaging, eroding trust, undermining self-esteem, and leading to feelings of confusion and helplessness. Victims often feel exploited, used, and abused. In some cases, manipulation is used by individuals or groups to gain power or control, such as in abusive relationships or cults.

Overall, manipulation is generally considered unethical and harmful. It is crucial to be aware of manipulative tactics and strive for open and honest communication in relationships. Romans 12:2 encourages us, "Do not conform to the pattern of this world, but be transformed by the renewing of your mind."

Types of Manipulation

Manipulators employ various aggressive and passive-aggressive tactics to control others. Here are some common methods:

- Sarcastic Swords: Stabbing with cutting humor, jabbing words, painful put-downs, or malicious mocking.

- Sly Suggestions: Making suggestions intended to make a person feel guilty.

- Slam/Bam Slamming: Slamming drawers, doors, phones, or books.

- Sizeable Sighs: Audible sighs, deep grunts, long groans, or smacked lips.

These behaviors are designed to make you feel guilty, indebted, or even crazy. Emotional manipulators are masters at leveraging guilt to their advantage. If you bring up an issue, they make you feel guilty for mentioning it. If you keep it to yourself, they make you feel guilty for not sharing.

Other manipulative behaviors include:

- Strategic Stalling: Intentionally slow, late, not hearing, or forgetful.

- Scheming Shoulds: Statements like "You should show me respect," or "You should make me happy."

- Sexy Seduction: Seductive talk, suggestive clothing, or sensual body movements.

- Strident Screaming: Yelling to unnerve, publicly humiliate, or personally intimidate.

- Showering Sentiments: Excessive praise or affection to gain an advantage.

- Sympathy Seekers: Acting needy with 'pity parties.'

- Silent Treatment: Pouting, brooding, or ignoring.

- Scorning Sneers: Curling the lip, raising eyebrows, squinting eyes.

- Sniveling Sobbers: Timed tears, subtle sniffers, tearful stories.

- Suppressed Support: Withholding compliments, gifts, affection, or presence.

These tactics are condemned by Scripture. For instance, Psalm 52:2 says, "Your tongue plots destruction; it is like a sharpened razor, you who practice deceit."

Why People Manipulate

People manipulate for various reasons:

- Avoiding Obligations: Dodging responsibilities.

- Maintaining Control: Keeping others 'hooked' into a relationship.

- Winning Control Battles: Dominating situations for personal gain.

Manipulation is a form of negotiation, control, or influence for one's own advantage. Proverbs 26:24-25 warns us, "Enemies disguise themselves with their lips, but in their hearts they harbor deceit. Though their speech is charming, do not believe them, for seven abominations fill their hearts."

Why People Allow Themselves to Be Manipulated

People allow manipulation for several reasons:

- Misplaced Identity: Believing they need the manipulator's approval to feel significant.

- Fear of Disapproval: Being afraid of neglect or rejection.

- Control by Personality or Power: Being controlled by what the manipulator does or threatens to do.

In such cases, repentance is essential. We must ask God to forgive us for coming under false authority. Ephesians 5:2 calls us to "walk in the way of love, just as Christ loved us and gave himself up for us as a fragrant offering and sacrifice to God." For freedom, Christ has set us free (Galatians 5:1).

Steps to Stop Being Manipulated

To stop being manipulated, one can:

1. Expect Exasperation: Don't expect the manipulator to understand or agree with your decisions. Matthew 5:37 says, "Let your yes be yes, and your no, no."

2. Prepare for Pain: Accept that change is painful but necessary. Confront the manipulator as 2 Timothy 1:7 encourages, "For the Spirit God gave us does not make us timid, but gives us power, love, and self-discipline."

3. Examine Methods: Ask God to open your eyes to the ways you've been manipulated and write out tactics for change. If necessary, cut ties with the manipulator (Revelation 2:21).

4. Nullify Needs: Realize that God didn't design anyone to meet all the needs of another person. Psalm 27:1 says, "The Lord is my light and my salvation—whom shall I fear? The Lord is the stronghold of my life—of whom shall I be afraid?"

Manipulation is a harmful behavior condemned by God's Word. By recognizing manipulative tactics, understanding why people manipulate, and taking steps to stop being manipulated, we can live in the freedom that Christ provides. Romans 12:21 reminds us, "Do not be overcome by evil, but overcome evil with good."

CHAPTER 30

Marriage: To Have and To Hold

Matthew 19:6 (NIV): "So they are no longer two, but one flesh. Therefore what God has joined together, let no one separate."

The Covenant of Marriage

Marriage is a sacred covenant where a man and woman are legally and spiritually united as husband and wife. This union is designed by God and serves as a reflection of His relationship with the church. Genesis 2:24-25 outlines the foundation of this covenant with four key elements.

Genesis 2:24-25 (NIV): "That is why a man leaves his father and mother and is united to his wife, and they become one flesh. Adam and his wife were both naked, and they felt no shame."

Elements of God's Perfect Order for Marriage

1. Separation: Leaving one's parents to form a new family unit is crucial. Failure to do so can lead to conflict and stress. This does not

mean ignoring parents but recognizing that the new marital relationship takes priority.

Ephesians 5:31 (NIV): "For this reason, a man will leave his father and mother and be united to his wife, and the two will become one flesh."

2. Bonding: The concept of "cleaving" emphasizes deep intimacy and unity. It means being joined to your spouse, and building a relationship that withstands hardships and flourishes in love.

Ecclesiastes 4:9-12 (NIV): "Two are better than one, because they have a good return for their labor: If either of them falls down, one can help the other up. But pity anyone who falls and has no one to help them up."

3. Oneness: Marriage brings two individuals together as one, blending their lives, dreams, and goals. This oneness is a powerful bond that mirrors our union with Christ.

4. Intimacy: Emotional and physical intimacy is vital for a thriving marriage. It fosters a deep connection and mutual understanding.

Types of Troubled Marriages

1. Make-Believe Marriage: This marriage lacks honest communication and intimacy. Couples avoid addressing problems and fail to acknowledge each other's feelings and needs.

Philippians 2:3 (NIV): "Do nothing out of selfish ambition or vain conceit. Rather, in humility value others above yourselves."

2. Maladjusted Marriage: Sexual difficulties arise from issues like frigidity, impatience, infidelity, fatigue, or anger. These problems often stem from unforgiveness and manipulation.

1 Corinthians 7:3-4 (NIV): "The husband should fulfill his marital duty to his wife, and likewise the wife to her husband. The wife does not have authority over her own body but yields it to her husband. In the same way, the husband does not have authority over his own body but yields it to his wife."

3. Mixed-Up Marriage: Power struggles, tension, and criticism prevail due to conflicting values, religious beliefs, and moral principles.

Philippians 2:2 (NIV): "Then make my joy complete by being like-minded, having the same love, being one in spirit and of one mind."

4. Money-Troubled Marriage: Financial disagreements over earning, spending, and budgeting cause strain and conflict.

Hebrews 13:5 (NIV): "Keep your lives free from the love of money and be content with what you have, because God has said, 'Never will I leave you; never will I forsake you.'"

5. Misaligned Marriage: Failure to recognize and fulfill God-given roles leads to dysfunction. Husbands neglect their spiritual leadership, and wives struggle with control issues.

Ephesians 5:22-23, 25 (NIV): "Wives, submit yourselves to your own husbands as you do to the Lord. For the husband is the head of the wife as Christ is the head of the church, his body, of which he is the Savior. Husbands, love your wives, just as Christ loved the church and gave himself up for her."

The Foundation of a Successful Marriage

Marriage is the most intimate human relationship, second only to our relationship with God. It often reveals both the best and worst in us. At the root of many marriage problems is selfishness. When partners prioritize their needs above their spouse's, conflict arises.

Matthew 19:6 (NIV): "So they are no longer two, but one flesh. Therefore what God has joined together, let no one separate."

Mark 10:8 (NIV): "And the two will become one flesh. So they are no longer two, but one flesh."

Addressing Unrealistic Expectations

Couples often enter marriage with unrealistic expectations, leading to disappointment and bitterness. Good advice for managing expectations includes gratitude and submission to God's will.

1 Thessalonians 5:18 (NIV): "Give thanks in all circumstances; for this is God's will for you in Christ Jesus."

Ephesians 5:21 (NIV): "Submit to one another out of reverence for Christ."

God-Given Inner Needs

All individuals have three God-given inner needs: love, significance, and security. Husbands often need significance, while wives seek security.

Philippians 2:4 (NIV): "Not looking to your own interests but each of you to the interests of the others."

Wives can fulfill their husband's needs by praising his character and reassuring him of his worth. Husbands can fulfill their wife's needs by offering emotional support, financial stability, and prioritizing their family.

Building a Strong Marriage: The C-O-V-E-N-A-N-T

C: Commit to working through problems, not walking away.

O: Offer love to your mate even when you don't feel like it.

V: View your marriage as God's setting for spiritual growth.

E: Eliminate any emphasis on your rights.

N: Nurture your identity in Christ.

A: Ask God to change you.

N: Nourish your extended family relationships.

T: Turn your expectations over to God.

God is the missing puzzle piece in many marriages today. A marriage focused on God offers guidance from the Bible on how to love one another and live out His will.

Genesis 1:31 (NIV): "God saw all that he had made, and it was very good."

When we ignore God's plan, we end up frustrated. The focus shifts to an unwritten contract where spouses maintain a list of expectations, leading to conflict and disappointment.

God's plan is for each spouse to submit to Christ and seek His purposes. A biblical marriage involves both partners submitting to Christ and striving to follow His will.

The Key to a Successful Marriage: Commitment

Commitment is the glue that holds a marriage together. When both spouses apply biblical truths and seek God's heart, there is no problem they cannot overcome.

Ephesians 5:25 (NIV): "Husbands, love your wives, just as Christ loved the church and gave himself up for her."

By making their relationship with God the primary focus, couples can navigate challenges and build a strong, enduring marriage.

CHAPTER 31

The Occult: Demystifying the Deeds of Darkness

Ephesians 5:11 (NIV): "Have nothing to do with the fruitless deeds of darkness, but rather expose them."

The word "occult" comes from the Latin word "occultus," which means "hidden" or "secret." It often refers to practices or beliefs involving the supernatural, mysticism, or esoteric knowledge. The occult can include practices such as divination, witchcraft, alchemy, and spiritualism. While some view the occult as a spiritual journey or a way to explore the unknown, others see it as dangerous and associated with negative, even demonic, forces.

Intrigue and Danger of the Occult

Because occult practices are shrouded in secrecy, they can intrigue individuals and draw them in. Often, involvement begins innocuously, such as playing with a Ouija board out of curiosity.

However, many who start with seemingly "harmless" activities find themselves deeper in the occult, much like quicksand—easy to enter but difficult to escape.

Deuteronomy 18:10-12 (NIV): "Let no one be found among you who sacrifices their son or daughter in the fire, who practices divination or sorcery, interprets omens, engages in witchcraft, or casts spells, or who is a medium or spiritist or who consults the dead. Anyone who does these things is detestable to the Lord."

Categories of the Occult

The occult is generally divided into five categories: Fortune-telling, Superstition, Spiritism, White and Black Magic, and Parapsychology. Each category encompasses various practices that seek to gain supernatural power, abilities, or knowledge apart from God. This fascination with the occult has persisted from ancient times to the present, captivating millions, regardless of their background or education.

Colossians 2:8 (NIV): "See to it that no one takes you captive through hollow and deceptive philosophy, which depends on human tradition and the elemental spiritual forces of this world rather than on Christ."

Divination: Attempting to Foretell the Future

Divination is an attempt to predict or divine the future. Practices include:

Astrology: This practice involves studying stars and planets to reveal their supposed influence on people and events. However, astrology faces several significant problems:

- Scientific Problem: Astrology is based on the ancient belief that the sun circles the earth, but science has proven that the earth circles the sun.

- Sociological Problem: Astrological readings are based on one's birth date and place, yet identical twins often have different futures.

- Biblical Problem: Astrology violates God's Word.

Isaiah 47:13-14 (NIV): "All the counsel you have received has only worn you out! Let your astrologers come forward, those stargazers who make predictions month by month, let them save you from what is coming upon you. Surely they are like stubble; the fire will burn them up. They cannot even save themselves from the power of the flame."

Other practices include cartomancy (reading tarot cards), horoscopes, numerology, palmistry, psychic games, rod and pendulum, scrying, sortilege, tasseography, and water witching.

Leviticus 19:31 (NIV): "Do not turn to mediums or seek out spiritists, for you will be defiled by them. I am the Lord your God."

Spiritism: Communicating with the Unseen World

Spiritism involves attempting to communicate with the spirit world. Practices include channeling, where a medium channels information from a deceased person to the living.

1 Timothy 2:5-6 (NIV): "For there is one God and one mediator between God and mankind, the man Christ Jesus, who gave himself as a ransom for all people."

Satanism and Witchcraft

Satanism involves the worship of Satan and often includes mocking Christianity and exalting evil. Witchcraft, often associated with casting spells and invoking spirits, is forbidden by God.

Exodus 22:18 (NIV): "Do not allow a sorceress to live."

Supernatural Phenomena and Deception

Clairvoyance, ESP, and other paranormal activities are counterfeits of God's work, empowered by Satan to deceive.

1 John 4:1 (NIV): "Dear friends, do not believe every spirit, but test the spirits to see whether they are from God because many false prophets have gone out into the world."

The Christian Response to the Occult

Christians are called to avoid all forms of the occult and rely on the power of Jesus Christ. The Bible strictly warns against engaging in these practices.

Ephesians 5:11 (NIV): "Have nothing to do with the fruitless deeds of darkness, but rather expose them."

Steps to Renouncing the Occult

If someone recognizes involvement in the occult, they should:

1. Renounce Involvement: Publicly denounce any association with occult practices.

Acts 19:18 (NIV): "Many of those who believed now came and openly confessed what they had done."

2. Remove Occult Objects: Get rid of all items related to the occult.

Acts 19:19 (NIV): "A number who had practiced sorcery brought their scrolls together and burned them publicly."

3. Recognize Satan as the Enemy: Understand that the true enemy is Satan.

1 Peter 5:8 (NIV): "Be alert and of sober mind. Your enemy the devil prowls around like a roaring lion looking for someone to devour."

4. Rely on Christ's Authority: Depend on the authority of Jesus Christ to overcome evil.

1 John 4:4 (NIV): "You, dear children, are from God and have overcome them, because the one who is in you is greater than the one who is in the world."

5. Refuse Fascination with the Occult: Reject any ongoing interest in the occult.

Deuteronomy 18:10-14 (NIV): "Let no one be found among you who sacrifices their son or daughter in the fire, who practices divination or sorcery, interprets omens, engages in witchcraft, or casts spells, or who is a medium or spiritist or who consults the dead. Anyone who does these things is detestable to the Lord."

6. Reside in Fellowship with Believers: Maintain close fellowship with other Christians.

2 Corinthians 6:14 (NIV): "Do not be yoked together with unbelievers. For what do righteousness and wickedness have in common? Or what fellowship can light have with darkness?"

7. Reap the Benefits of Earnest Prayer: Engage in fervent and effective prayer.

James 5:16 (NIV): "The prayer of a righteous person is powerful and effective."

The Bible is clear that involvement in the occult is forbidden and dangerous. Christians must be vigilant, rejecting these practices and embracing the power and authority of Jesus Christ to overcome evil. By understanding and obeying God's Word, we can stand firm against the deeds of darkness and walk in the light of His truth.

CHAPTER 32

Overeating: Freedom from Food Fixation

Philippians 3:19 (NIV): "Their destiny is destruction, their god is their stomach, and their glory is in their shame. Their mind is set on earthly things."

Gluttony: A Sin Often Ignored

Gluttony is the excessive consumption of food and drink, leading to overindulgence or waste. It is considered one of the seven deadly sins in many religious traditions, including Christianity, Judaism, and Islam. The effects of gluttony are both physical and psychological, and they can be severely detrimental. Physically, overeating can cause obesity, high blood pressure, diabetes, heart disease, liver damage, and gastrointestinal issues. The Bible warns us about the dangers of overindulgence. Proverbs 23:20-21 (NIV) cautions, "Do not join those who drink too much wine or gorge themselves on meat, for drunkards and gluttons become poor, and drowsiness clothes them in rags."

The Psychological and Social Impact of Gluttony

Psychologically, gluttony leads to guilt, shame, and a loss of self-control, contributing to low self-esteem and poor mental health. It can even lead to eating disorders such as binge eating disorder, bulimia nervosa, and anorexia nervosa. Proverbs 25:16 (NIV) advises moderation: "If you find honey, eat just enough—too much of it, and you will vomit." Furthermore, gluttony has social and environmental consequences, contributing to food waste and depleting natural resources. It also increases healthcare costs and exacerbates economic disparities.

Compulsive Eating: A Form of Addiction

Compulsive eating is an irresistible impulse to eat, defined as uncontrolled eating that can result in physical disorders. It often leads to obesity, a condition marked by excessive body fat. Gluttony is a sin that Christians frequently overlook, often condemning smoking and drinking while ignoring their own overeating habits. Matthew 7:3-5 (NIV) reminds us of the importance of self-reflection: "Why do you look at the speck of sawdust in your brother's eye and pay no attention to the plank in your eye?"

The Biblical Perspective on Gluttony

In Scripture, gluttony is seen as a loss of control and yielding to fleshly desires instead of yielding to God. Proverbs 23:2 (NIV) starkly warns, "Put a knife to your throat if you are given to gluttony." This emphasizes the severity of the issue, noting that both gluttony and drunkenness lead to poverty. Money is a God-given resource meant to sustain us and build His kingdom, not to be squandered on overindulgence.

Physical and Emotional Symptoms of Overeating

Physical symptoms of compulsive overeating include chronic pain, high blood pressure, diabetes, heart disease, and shortness of breath. Emotional symptoms include low self-esteem, depression, guilt, powerlessness, and hopelessness. 1 Corinthians 6:19-20 (NIV) underscores the importance of treating our bodies with respect: "Do you not know that your bodies are temples of the Holy Spirit, who is in you, whom you have received from God? You are not your own; you were bought at a price. Therefore, honor God with your bodies."

Causes and Triggers of Overeating

Overeating often stems from emotional needs such as seeking significance, security, or unconditional love. Poor eating habits established in childhood, depression, and substituting one addictive behavior for another can also be triggers. Eating disorders often arise from a combination of chemical imbalances, stress, and negative self-view. Psalm 34:17-18 (NIV) offers comfort: "The righteous cry out, and the Lord hears them; he delivers them from all their troubles. The Lord is close to the brokenhearted and saves those who are crushed in spirit."

Overcoming Overeating with God's Help

To overcome overeating, individuals must recognize the emotional roots of their behavior and commit to change. 1 Peter 5:7 (NIV) encourages us to, "Cast all your anxiety on him because he cares for you." This includes identifying emotional triggers and seeking fulfillment in God, not food. Changing eating habits through the power of Christ within us is crucial. Philippians 4:13 (NIV) assures us, "I can do all this through him who gives me strength."

Steps to Freedom from Food Fixation

1. Commit to Obey God: Recognize the powerlessness over food and the need for God's help. 1 John 3:24 (NIV): "The one who keeps God's commands lives in him, and he in them. And this is how we know that he lives in us: We know it by the Spirit he gave us."

2. Recognize Emotional Hunger: Differentiate between physical and emotional hunger. Only God can meet emotional needs. Psalm 107:9 (NIV): "For he satisfies the thirsty and fills the hungry with good things."

3. Nurture Your Relationship with God: Pray, meditate on Scripture, and remember God's power over temptation. 2 Peter 1:3-4 (NIV): "His divine power has given us everything we need for a godly life through our knowledge of him who called us by his own glory and goodness."

4. Make Wise Choices: Choose to glorify God with your body and reject the urge to overeat. 1 Corinthians 10:31 (NIV): "So whether you eat or drink or whatever you do, do it all for the glory of God."

Daily Affirmations for Overcoming Overeating

If you counsel someone battling with overeating, these daily affirmations can help:

- I choose to change my eating habits through the power of Christ within me.

- I choose to live to please God, not to please my appetite.

- I choose to make wise choices when tempted to eat unwisely.

- I choose to make the right choices when tempted to eat excessively.

- I choose to glorify God and reflect Him through my body.

- I choose to focus not on food, but on faithfulness to the Lord in my life.

- I choose to let God be my God, not to let food be my god.

- Although I've failed in the past, with God's help, I don't have to fail in the future.

Psalm 73:26 (NIV): "My flesh and my heart may fail, but God is the strength of my heart and my portion forever." With God's help, we can overcome the struggle of overeating and live a life that honors Him.

Parenting: Step for Successful Parenting

Matthew 19:14 (NIV): "Jesus said, 'Let the little children come to me, and do not hinder them, for the kingdom of heaven belongs to such as these.'"

Understanding Different Parenting Styles

People parent their children differently, and these methods significantly affect a child's development and behavior. There are five main parenting styles:

1. Domineering: These parents seek to control a child's behavior. They tend to think in black and white terms and may be controlling, inflexible, critical, and performance-oriented. Ephesians 6:4 (NIV) instructs, "Fathers, do not exasperate your children; instead, bring them up in the training and instruction of the Lord."

2. Doting: These parents seek to control a child's feelings. They yield easily to pressure in their desperation to achieve harmony in their family. They tend to be overprotective and overly involved. This type

of parent can also be referred to as a "helicopter parent." Proverbs 13:24 (NIV) states, "Whoever spares the rod hates their children, but the one who loves their children is careful to discipline them."

3. Dependent: These parents seek to control both the child's behavior and feelings. They are often manipulative, possessive, suspicious, inconsistent, and controlling. Philippians 4:19 (NIV) says, "And my God will meet all your needs according to the riches of his glory in Christ Jesus."

4. Detached: These parents avoid responsibility for the child's failures. They lack boundaries and follow-through, tending to be apathetic, ambivalent, and uninvolved. Proverbs 29:15 (NIV) teaches, "The rod of correction imparts wisdom, but a child left undisciplined disgraces its mother."

5. Developing: These parents aim to teach a child and develop their character. They are loving, encouraging, comforting, and sincere. Proverbs 22:6 (NIV) encourages, "Start children off on the way they should go, and even when they are old, they will not turn from it."

The Impact of Parenting Styles

- Dependent Parents: Their children tend to become fearful, deceitful, jealous, indecisive, and passive.

- Domineering Parents: Their children often become rebellious, fearful of failure, overly sensitive to criticism, bitter, underachievers, or overachievers.

- Developing Parents: Their children typically become secure, confident, compassionate, honest, and wise.

- Detached Parents: Their children may become self-sufficient, emotionally hardened, rebellious, insecure, and underachievers.

- Doting Parents: Their children tend to become spoiled, manipulative, disrespectful, irresponsible, and helpless.

Ephesians 6:1-3 (NIV) advises, "Children, obey your parents in the Lord, for this is right. 'Honor your father and mother'—which is the first commandment with a promise—'so that it may go well with you and that you may enjoy long life on the earth.'"

Effective Discipline: Expressing Love Through Limits

Discipline is training that corrects, molds, and improves a child's character. It is an expression of love and acceptance that builds a sense of security in a child. Hebrews 12:11 (NIV) explains, "No discipline seems pleasant at the time, but painful. Later on, however, it produces a harvest of righteousness and peace for those who have been trained by it."

The 'Don'ts' of Effective Discipline:

1. Don't feel guilty when you discipline your child. You show love by setting limits. Proverbs 13:24 (NIV): "Whoever spares the rod hates their children, but the one who loves their children is careful to discipline them."

2. Don't be afraid of losing your child's love. Doing God's will earns respect. Hebrews 12:6 (NIV): "Because the Lord disciplines the one he loves, and he chastens everyone he accepts as his son."

3. Don't view structure and limits as punishment. Establish beneficial boundaries. 1 Corinthians 14:40 (NIV): "But everything should be done in a fitting and orderly way."

4. Don't embarrass your child in front of others. Praise in public, correct in private. Ephesians 4:29 (NIV): "Do not let any unwholesome talk come out of your mouths, but only what is helpful for building others up according to their needs."

5. Don't belittle your child with sarcasm. Speak the truth in love. Proverbs 15:1 (NIV): "A gentle answer turns away wrath, but a harsh word stirs up anger."

6. Don't discipline in anger. Wait for anger to pass, and pray for wisdom. James 1:20 (NIV): "Because human anger does not produce the righteousness that God desires."

7. Don't manipulate with fear or guilt. Base appeals on a clear conscience before God. 1 John 3:21 (NIV): "Dear friends, if our hearts do not condemn us, we have confidence before God."

8. Don't compare your child with others. See them as unique creations of God. Psalm 139:14 (NIV): "I praise you because I am fearfully and wonderfully made; your works are wonderful, I know that full well."

The 'Do's' of Effective Discipline

1. Mold the will without breaking the spirit. Treat the child with kindness and respect. Colossians 3:21 (NIV): "Fathers, do not embitter your children, or they will become discouraged."

2. Communicate expectations clearly. Get at the child's eye level, describe expectations, and give gentle reminders. 1 Thessalonians 4:1 (NIV): "As for other matters, brothers and sisters, we instructed you how to live in order to please God, as in fact you are living. Now we ask you and urge you in the Lord Jesus to do this more and more."

3. Establish and enforce negative consequences for misbehavior. Make consequences related to the behavior and clearly communicated. Proverbs 19:18 (NIV): "Discipline your children, for in that there is hope; do not be a willing party to their death."

4. Encourage and develop responsibility. Allow choices and experiences of their consequences. Galatians 6:7 (NIV): "Do not be deceived: God cannot be mocked. A man reaps what he sows."

5. Assign beneficial chores based on capabilities. Ensure everyone has roles and responsibilities. 1 Corinthians 12:12 (NIV): "Just as a body, though one, has many parts, but all its many parts form one body, so it is with Christ."

6. Reinforce positive behavior. Offer smiles, physical affection, and praise. Proverbs 3:27 (NIV): "Do not withhold good from those to whom it is due, when it is in your power to act."

7. Maintain consistency. Evaluate and modify rules as your child grows, present a united front in public, and resolve disagreements

in private. James 1:5 (NIV): "If any of you lacks wisdom, you should ask God, who gives generously to all without finding fault, and it will be given to you."

Wise Parenting Strategies

1. Nurture God's character in your child. Love and listen attentively with your ears and heart. James 1:19 (NIV): "My dear brothers and sisters, take note of this: Everyone should be quick to listen, slow to speak, and slow to become angry."

2. Organize your family God's way. Involve your children in church and ministry. Proverbs 1:8 (NIV): "Listen, my son, to your father's instruction and do not forsake your mother's teaching."

3. Love your spouse openly and unconditionally. This models healthy relationships. Ephesians 5:33 (NIV): "However, each one of you also must love his wife as he loves himself, and the wife must respect her husband."

4. Refuse to show favoritism. Treat each child as unique. James 2:1 (NIV): "My brothers and sisters, believers in our glorious Lord Jesus Christ must not show favoritism."

5. Encourage and affirm each child daily. Psalm 127:3 (NIV): "Children are a heritage from the Lord, offspring a reward from him."

6. Model repentance and forgiveness. Matthew 5:23-24 (NIV): "Therefore, if you are offering your gift at the altar and there remember that your brother or sister has something against you, leave your gift there in front of the altar. First go and be reconciled to them; then come and offer your gift."

7. Establish age-appropriate boundaries. 1 Thessalonians 4:1 (NIV): "As for other matters, brothers and sisters, we instructed you how to live in order to please God, as in fact you are living. Now we ask you and urge you in the Lord Jesus to do this more and more."

8. Enforce boundaries consistently. Proverbs 19

:18 (NIV): "Discipline your children, for in that there is hope; do not be a willing party to their death."

9. Deal appropriately with strong emotions. Colossians 3:8 (NIV): "But now you must also rid yourselves of all such things as these: anger, rage, malice, slander, and filthy language from your lips."

10. Base discipline on love, not anger. Revelation 3:19 (NIV): "Those whom I love I rebuke and discipline. So be earnest and repent."

Proverbs 22:6 (NIV): "Start children off on the way they should go, and even when they are old, they will not turn from it." Godly parenting is essential today. Fathers and mothers are the key to raising godly young men and women who love God and live for Him. Despite the blessing of pastors, youth leaders, and other godly influences, no one can replace the role of godly parents who live out their Christian faith and pass it on to their children. This is why Proverbs 22:6 rightly claims, "Start children off on the way they should go, and even when they are old, they will not turn from it."

CHAPTER 34

Phobias: No Longer Afraid

Isaiah 41:10 (NIV): "Do not fear, for I am with you; do not be dismayed, for I am your God. I will strengthen you and help you; I will uphold you with my righteous right hand."

A phobia is an extreme and irrational fear of a particular object, situation, or activity. It is a type of anxiety disorder that can significantly impact a person's daily life and well-being. This intense fear is not just an ordinary worry; it paralyzes and overwhelms the individual.

2 Timothy 1:7 (NIV): "For God has not given us a spirit of fear, but of power and of love and of a sound mind." This scripture reminds us that fear is not from God but from the enemy, and we must confront it with the power and love given to us by the Holy Spirit.

Phobias can take many forms and can be triggered by a wide range of stimuli, such as spiders, heights, enclosed spaces, flying, or public speaking. When a person encounters the object or situation that triggers their phobia, they may experience intense feelings of fear, panic, and anxiety, often accompanied by physical symptoms such as sweating, shaking, and a rapid heartbeat. These reactions are the body's fight-or-flight response in overdrive.

Psalm 34:4 (NIV): "I sought the Lord, and he answered me; he delivered me from all my fears." When we seek God earnestly, He is faithful to deliver us from our fears, providing peace that surpasses understanding.

Phobias are typically diagnosed when the fear is persistent and excessive, leading to significant distress and impairment in social, occupational, or other important areas of functioning. Treatment for phobias may involve therapy, medication, or a combination of both. Cognitive-behavioral therapy (CBT) is a common approach that helps individuals identify and challenge negative thoughts and beliefs that contribute to their phobia, while also gradually exposing them to the feared stimulus in a controlled environment. This therapeutic process is much like renewing our minds with God's truth.

Romans 12:2 (NIV): "Do not conform to the pattern of this world but be transformed by the renewing of your mind. Then you will be able to test and approve what God's will is—his good, pleasing and perfect will." Transforming our minds with God's truth is essential in overcoming irrational fears.

Examples of Phobias

1. Specific Phobias (Simple Phobias): Persistent excessive fear when in the presence of, or in the anticipated presence of, a specific object or situation. Psalm 27:1 (NIV): "The Lord is my light and my salvation—whom shall I fear? The Lord is the stronghold of my life—of whom shall I be afraid?"

2. Social Phobias (Social Anxiety Disorder): Paralyzing fear of appearing stupid or being judged as shameful in a social situation. Philippians 4:6-7 (NIV): "Do not be anxious about anything, but in every situation, by prayer and petition, with thanksgiving, present your

requests to God. And the peace of God, which transcends all understanding, will guard your hearts and your minds in Christ Jesus."

3. Agoraphobia: Fear of open spaces or fear of fear itself, often due to the fear of having a panic attack in a place where escape could be difficult or embarrassing. Isaiah 41:13 (NIV): "For I am the Lord your God who takes hold of your right hand and says to you, Do not fear; I will help you."

Overcoming Hyperventilation

Hyperventilation is shallow, rapid breathing that reduces carbon dioxide in the blood, leading to lightheadedness, dizziness, tingling in the extremities, palpitations, and feelings of faintness and respiratory distress. This often accompanies anxiety and phobia attacks.

Philippians 4:8 (NIV): "Finally, brothers and sisters, whatever is true, whatever is noble, whatever is right, whatever is pure, whatever is lovely, whatever is admirable—if anything is excellent or praiseworthy—think about such things." Redirecting our thoughts to what is true and noble can help calm our anxiety.

When you hyperventilate, you do not give your body long enough to retain CO_2, and so your body cannot use the oxygen you have. Sometimes, breathing into a paper bag can help restore the balance of CO_2 and oxygen.

Key Contributors to Irrational Fear: F.E.A.R.

1. Former Experiences: Traumatic experiences can set the stage for phobias. Psalm 34:17-18 (NIV): "The righteous cry out, and the Lord hears them; he delivers them from all their troubles. The Lord is close to the brokenhearted and saves those who are crushed in spirit."

2. Emotional Overload: Stress and overwhelming emotions contribute to irrational fears. Matthew 11:28-30 (NIV): "Come to me, all you who are weary and burdened, and I will give you rest. Take my yoke upon you and learn from me, for I am gentle and humble in heart,

and you will find rest for your souls. For my yoke is easy and my burden is light."

3. Avoidance of Threatening Situations: Avoidance can reinforce phobias, making them more intense. Joshua 1:9 (NIV): "Have I not commanded you? Be strong and courageous. Do not be afraid; do not be discouraged, for the Lord your God will be with you wherever you go."

4. Runaway Imagination: Anticipating the worst and believing it will never change. Philippians 4:8 (NIV): Encourages us to focus on what is true, noble, and right, rather than on fear and negativity.

Steps to Desensitization

1. Systematic Repetition: Gradually face the fear, one step at a time. Psalm 56:3-4 (NIV): "When I am afraid, I put my trust in you. In God, whose word I praise—in God I trust and am not afraid. What can mere mortals do to me?"

2. Consistent Practice: Repeat the same step daily until anxiety decreases. James 1:4 (NIV): "Let perseverance finish its work so that you may be mature and complete, not lacking anything."

3. Gradual Progression: Expect anxiety when moving to the next step, but know it will dissipate with increased repetition. Isaiah 40:31 (NIV): "But those who hope in the Lord will renew their strength. They will soar on wings like eagles; they will run and not grow weary, they will walk and not be faint."

The Path to Recovery

The Lord wants to lead you out of fear and into faith, trusting in His strong protective hand rather than the flimsy refuge of your fear-lined ditch walls. Psalm 23 (NIV) is a powerful passage to meditate on, helping us to exchange panic for peace.

1. Psalm 23:1-6 (NIV): "The Lord is my shepherd, I lack nothing. He makes me lie down in green pastures, he leads me beside quiet waters, he refreshes my soul. He guides me along the right paths for his name's sake. Even though I walk through the darkest valley, I

will fear no evil, for you are with me; your rod and your staff, they comfort me. You prepare a table before me in the presence of my enemies. You anoint my head with oil; my cup overflows. Surely your goodness and love will follow me all the days of my life, and I will dwell in the house of the Lord forever."

This passage reminds us that God is our Shepherd, guiding us through dark valleys and leading us to peace and safety. With His rod and staff, He comforts and protects us, ensuring we lack nothing. Even in the presence of our enemies, He provides for us abundantly.

Romans 8:15 (NIV): "The Spirit you received does not make you slaves so that you live in fear again; rather, the Spirit you received brought about your adoption to sonship. And by him, we cry, 'Abba, Father.'" This verse assures us of our identity in Christ and our freedom from the bondage of fear.

CHAPTER 35

Pregnancy- Unplanned: I'm Pregnant

Jeremiah 1:5 (NIV): "Before I formed you in the womb, I knew you, before you were born, I set you apart."

An unplanned pregnancy can bring a whirlwind of emotions and uncertainty. But it's crucial to remember that God's heart is deeply invested in every unborn child. He is the Author of life and has a purpose for every being He creates. Deuteronomy 32:39 (NIV): "See now that I am He! There is no god besides me. I put to death and I bring to life, I have wounded and I will heal, and no one can deliver out of my hand." This verse emphasizes God's ultimate control over life and death, reassuring us of His sovereignty in every situation.

God's Heart for the Unborn

Psalm 139:13-16 (NIV): "For you created my inmost being; you knit me together in my mother's womb. I praise you because I am fearfully and wonderfully made; your works are wonderful, I know that full well. My frame was not hidden from you when I was made in the secret place, when I was woven together in the depths of the earth. Your eyes saw my unformed body; all the days ordained for me were written in your book before one of them came to be." God is intricately involved in the formation of every life, highlighting the sanctity and purpose of each individual.

Genesis 29:31 (NIV): "When the Lord saw that Leah was not loved, he enabled her to conceive, but Rachel remained childless." and 1 Samuel 1:5 (NIV): "But to Hannah, he gave a double portion because he loved her, and the Lord had closed her womb." These verses remind us that God opens and closes the womb according to His divine plan and wisdom.

Isaiah 44:24 (NIV): "This is what the Lord says—your Redeemer, who formed you in the womb: I am the Lord, the Maker of all things, who stretches out the heavens, who spread out the earth by myself." Every pregnancy, regardless of the circumstances, is ordained by God, affirming His role as the Creator of all life.

Jeremiah 29:11 (NIV): "For I know the plans I have for you," declares the Lord, "plans to prosper you and not to harm you, plans to give you hope and a future." God never forms a life without having a purpose for that life. His plans are always for our good, even when we can't see it.

Predictable Reactions to Unplanned Pregnancies

Women facing unplanned pregnancies often experience denial, dilemma, dread, depression, and distress. But from God's perspective, life begins at conception. Genesis 1:11, 24, 28 (NIV): "Then God said, 'Let the land produce vegetation: seed-bearing plants and trees on the land that bear fruit with seed in it, according to their various kinds.' And it was so. And God said, 'Let the land produce living creatures according to their kinds: livestock, creatures that move along the ground, and wild animals, each according to its kind.' And it was so.

God blessed them and said to them, 'Be fruitful and increase in number; fill the earth and subdue it.'" These verses establish the principle that all living things reproduce after their kind, affirming that a fetus is a human being from the moment of conception.

Considering the Options

Terminating a pregnancy adds guilt to grief. Proverbs 31:15 (NIV): "She gets up while it is still night; she provides food for her family and portions for her female servants." Single parenting is a significant commitment, involving physical, emotional, and spiritual nurturing.

Amos 3:3 (NIV): "Do two walk together unless they have agreed to do so?" Marriage should not be based solely on an unplanned pregnancy but on shared commitments, goals, and values.

Adoption: An Expression of Love

Adoption reflects the loving relationship of God with all who accept Jesus Christ as their Lord and Savior. Romans 8:15 (NIV): "The Spirit you received does not make you slaves so that you live in fear again; rather, the Spirit you received brought about your adoption to sonship. And by him, we cry, 'Abba, Father.'" Adoption into God's family is the ultimate expression of love and acceptance.

Making Wise Decisions

Making a quick decision can result in long-term grief. James 1:5 (NIV): "If any of you lacks wisdom, you should ask God, who gives generously to all without finding fault, and it will be given to you." Steps to take action with WISDOM:

1. Write down your thoughts and feelings: Admit your anxiety, confess any guilt, and cast your cares on the Lord. 1 Peter 5:7 (NIV): "Cast all your anxiety on him because he cares for you."

2. Imagine life for you and your baby: Consider short-term (next year) and long-term (ten years) implications of each option (abortion, parenting, adoption). Proverbs 16:9 (NIV): "In their hearts, humans plan their course, but the Lord establishes their steps."

3. Sort through your options: Evaluate them in light of God's revelations about your baby's life and what is best for your child. Psalm 32:8 (NIV): "I will instruct you and teach you in the way you should go; I will counsel you with my loving eye on you."

4. Develop a support structure: Lean on family and friends. Ecclesiastes 4:9-10 (NIV): "Two are better than one, because they have a good return for their labor: If either of them falls down, one can help the other up. But pity anyone who falls and has no one to help them up."

5. Obtain counsel aligned with God's Word: Proverbs 19:20-21 (NIV): "Listen to advice and accept discipline, and at the end you will be counted among the wise. Many are the plans in a person's heart, but it is the Lord's purpose that prevails."

6. Make a decision: Entrust your future and your baby's future into the hands of the Lord. Proverbs 3:5-6 (NIV): "Trust in the Lord with all your heart and lean not on your own understanding; in all your ways submit to him, and he will make your paths straight."

An unplanned pregnancy may seem like a crisis, but it is not a surprise to God. Jeremiah 29:11 (NIV): "For I know the plans I have for you," declares the Lord, "plans to prosper you and not to harm you, plans to give you hope and a future." God has a plan for you and your baby, and He will guide you through this challenging time.

CHAPTER 36
Prejudice: Pulling Up the Roots of Pride

"Woe to those who are wise in their own eyes." (Isaiah 5:21)

Understanding Prejudice

Prejudice is a preconceived opinion, usually unfavorable, formed without sufficient knowledge or just grounds. It is a negative attitude or belief towards a group of people based on their perceived characteristics, such as race, ethnicity, religion, gender, sexual orientation, or socioeconomic status, without any valid reason or evidence to support it. This unjustifiable bias can lead to discriminatory behavior and unfair treatment toward individuals or groups. Prejudice is an unfair and unreasonable opinion or feeling formed without enough thought or knowledge of the facts.

Categories of Prejudice

We tend to categorize people based on differences that place them into certain groups, often leading to prejudice. These categories can include:

- Age, Gender, Marital Status, Race, Appearance
- Disability, Income, Education, Intelligence
- Nationality, Religion, Social Class, Income

Today, stereotyping and prejudice are rampant in society. Common stereotypes include: all-powerful, career-driven women are single and lonely; all Latinos are here illegally; all Muslims are terrorists; all white people are racist; all Christians are Bible-thumping fanatics; all African Americans are on welfare; all New Yorkers are rude; and all politicians or lawyers are crooks. We habitually lump individuals of a certain race, class, or occupation into one category.

James 2:9 (NIV): "If you show favoritism, you sin and are convicted by the law as lawbreakers." Favoritism, in any form, is a sin because it reflects a judgmental attitude that goes against God's law of love and impartiality.

Root Causes of Prejudice

The root cause of prejudice often stems from wrong beliefs. A right belief, for someone struggling with prejudice, acknowledges that God does not show favoritism toward anyone. When we show prejudice toward others, we place ourselves as judges higher than God Himself.

Romans 15:7 (NIV): "Accept one another, then, just as Christ accepted you, in order to bring praise to God." This verse emphasizes the need for acceptance and love towards all, as Christ has accepted us.

Examining the Heart to Overcome Prejudice

To begin accepting others who are different, we must examine our hearts, thoughts, and motives. Here are some "Do's" and "Don'ts" for overcoming prejudice:

Don't judge the heart of another. (Matthew 7:1): This verse warns against judgment, reminding us that only God can judge the hearts and motives of individuals.

- We break this command when we think the worst of others.

- We break this command when we only speak of others' faults.

- We break this command when we judge an entire life by its worst moments.

- We break this command when we judge the hidden motives of others.

- We break this command when we judge others without considering their perspective.

- We break this command when we judge others without being mindful of our own judgment.

- We break this command when we judge others by superficial criteria like race, gender, or financial situation.

Do ask God to search your heart. (Psalm 139:23-24): Inviting God to examine our hearts can reveal hidden prejudices and help us seek His guidance in overcoming them.

Don't judge by outward appearances. (1 Samuel 16:7): God looks at the heart, not outward appearances. We must strive to do the same.

Do see and seek to meet the needs of others. (Philippians 2:4): Actively seeking to understand and meet the needs of others helps us develop empathy and compassion.

Don't use derogatory names or terms. (Titus 3:1-2): Speak evil of no one and always strive to show Christian kindness.

Do ask God to season your speech with His love. (Ephesians 4:29): Our words should always reflect God's love and grace.

Demonstrating Equality in Our Hearts

To show equality in our hearts, we must:

Express God's perspective on the equality of all people. (Galatians 3:28): "There is neither Jew nor Gentile, neither slave nor free, nor is there male and female, for you are all one in Christ Jesus."

Quit the tendency to stereotype. (James 2:1): "My brothers and sisters, believers in our glorious Lord Jesus Christ must not show favoritism."

Understand the God-given worth of all human beings. (Genesis 1:27): "So God created mankind in his own image, in the image of God he created them; male and female he created them."

Acknowledge your need for forgiveness and to forgive. (Colossians 3:13): "Bear with each other and forgive one another if any of you has a grievance against someone. Forgive as the Lord forgave you."

Learn that prejudice is irrational and emotional, not rational. (1 John 2:9, 11): "Anyone who claims to be in the light but hates a brother or sister is still in the darkness. But anyone who hates a brother or sister is in the darkness and walks around in the darkness."

Invest in others with a servant's heart. (Mark 10:45): "For even the Son of Man did not come to be served, but to serve, and to give his life as a ransom for many."

Turn from judging others to self-evaluation. (Matthew 7:4): "How can you say to your brother, 'Let me take the speck out of your eye,' when all the time there is a plank in your own eye?"

Yield in obedience to Christ's nature within you. (2 Peter 1:3-4): "His divine power has given us everything we need for a godly life through our knowledge of him who called us by his own glory and goodness. Through these he has given us his very great and precious promises, so that through them you may participate in the divine nature."

The Solution to Prejudice

The problem of prejudice is ultimately the sin of superiority. The solution for prejudice is undeniably living with Christ-like humility.

John 13:34 (NIV): "A new command I give you: Love one another. As I have loved you, so you must love one another." If God is impartial and loves us with impartiality, we need to love others with the same high standard.

Matthew 25:40 (NIV): "The King will reply, 'Truly I tell you, whatever you did for one of the least of these brothers and sisters of mine, you did for me.'" If we treat others with contempt, we are mistreating someone created in God's image and hurting someone whom God loves and for whom Jesus died.

Let us strive to pull up the roots of pride and prejudice in our hearts and replace them with Christ's love and humility.

CHAPTER 37

Premarital Counseling: Are You Fit to Be Tied?

"Above all else, guard your heart, for it is the wellspring of life." (Proverbs 4:23)

The Importance of Premarital Counseling

Premarital counseling is a form of therapy designed to help engaged couples prepare for marriage by addressing and resolving potential issues and conflicts that may arise in their relationship. It involves sessions with a trained therapist or counselor who works with the couple to identify and address areas of potential concern, such as communication, conflict resolution, values, goals, and expectations. The goal of premarital counseling is to help couples establish a strong and healthy foundation for their marriage and increase their chances of having a long and satisfying relationship.

Understanding Expectations and Desires

A couple needs to have an accurate understanding of each other's expectations and desires. Preparation for partnership is an excellent exercise for opening the door to meaningful communication. It is especially beneficial to do this with the guidance of a faith-based premarital counselor. The apostle Paul, in his pastoral instructions to Titus, told him to equip others who would, in turn, teach the younger generation (Titus 2:1–6). This is crucial in a premarital setting, as Biblical premarital counseling has at its core the teaching of biblical principles concerning marriage. The couple must be instructed in God's viewpoint on marriage.

Key Questions for Premarital Counseling

Both parties should complete a list of sentences in writing and then discuss each point. Questions that the counselor may ask the couple to consider in preparation for the partnership include:

- My definition of love and my reason for marriage is....

- My way of handling conflict and dealing with anger is....

- My debt history and my commitment regarding debt and saving is....

Premarital counseling is an excellent venue to raise issues the couple may not have considered, such as managing finances, splitting household chores, handling holidays, and disciplining children. The counselor can also guide the couple in identifying what they saw in their parents' marriages and what they want to imitate or avoid in their own marriage.

Contemplating Marriage

When contemplating marriage, individuals should consider:

- Don't live in your past. Look for the positive in the present. (Isaiah 43:18-19): "Forget the former things; do not dwell on the past. See, I am doing a new thing!"

- Don't focus on your future mate's past mistakes. Focus on your future mate's choice to marry you. (Proverbs 10:12): "Hatred stirs up conflict, but love covers over all wrongs."

- Don't expect to change your future mate. Accept your future mates the way they are. (Romans 15:7): "Accept one another, then, just as Christ accepted you, in order to bring praise to God."

Realistic Expectations

- Don't expect your future mate to meet all your needs. Expect God to be your primary need-meeter. (Philippians 4:19): "And my God will meet all your needs according to the riches of his glory in Christ Jesus."

- Don't nag your future mate. Make your position clear, then commit the matter to prayer. (Proverbs 19:13): "A quarrelsome wife is like the constant dripping of a leaky roof."

Agreement in Marriage

Amos 3:3 (NIV): "Do two walk together unless they have agreed to do so?" Couples should agree on a plan of action:

- We agree to first go to God with our problem, then seek guidance from God's Word.

- We agree to negotiate a solution, and then make a joint list of all options.

- We agree, if all options cancel out, to delay making a decision until there is unity or until a decision must be made. Trust in the sovereignty of God.

Romans 8:28 (NIV): "And we know that in all things God works for the good of those who love him, who have been called according to his purpose."

Spiritual Commitments

The couple should make commitments to grow spiritually together:

- Commit your lives to Jesus Christ and submit to His control. (Luke 9:23): "Whoever wants to be my disciple must deny themselves and take up their cross daily and follow me."

- Commit your home to God and make it Christ-centered. (Joshua 24:15): "But as for me and my household, we will serve the LORD."

- Commit your bodies to each other and vow to be sexually faithful. (Hebrews 13:4): "Marriage should be honored by all, and the marriage bed kept pure, for God will judge the adulterer and all the sexually immoral."

Sexual faithfulness in a godly marriage includes more than just physical faithfulness; it also involves emotional and mental fidelity. Keeping one's mind and heart devoted to their spouse helps in maintaining a pure and faithful relationship.

- Commit your finances to God and honor Him with your tithe. (Malachi 3:10): "Bring the whole tithe into the storehouse, that there may be food in my house. Test me in this," says the LORD Almighty, "and see if I will not throw open the floodgates of heaven and pour out so much blessing that there will not be room enough to store it."

- Commit to reading the Bible and praying together daily. (Psalm 119:105): "Your word is a lamp for my feet, a light on my path."

- Commit to not going to bed while still angry with one another. (Ephesians 4:26): "In your anger do not sin: Do not let the sun go down while you are still angry."

- Commit to nurturing each other through loving encouragement. (Hebrews 10:24): "And let us consider how we may spur one another on toward love and good deeds."

- Commit to admitting weaknesses and seeking prayer support to change. (James 5:16): "Therefore confess your sins to each other and pray for each other so that you may be healed. The prayer of a righteous person is powerful and effective."

- Commit to growing together in a deeper relationship with the Lord. (Hebrews 10:22): "Let us draw near to God with a sincere heart and with the full assurance that faith brings, having our hearts sprinkled to cleanse us from a guilty conscience and having our bodies washed with pure water."

Observing Relationship Dynamics

Two questions that might be excellent predictors of the future relationship of a couple are: "How does he treat his mother?" or "How does she treat her father?" Observing these interactions can reveal qualities such as respect, kindness, and willingness to listen—qualities that often carry over into the marriage relationship.

Proverbs 23:22 (NIV): "Listen to your father, who gave you life, and do not despise your mother when she is old." This verse underscores the importance of respect and care within family relationships.

Reflecting Christ's Love

The Bible tells us that marriage is to reflect the sacrificial love that Christ had for His bride, the church:

Ephesians 5:21, 33 (NIV): "Submit to one another out of reverence for Christ... Each one of you also must love his wife as he loves himself, and the wife must respect her husband."

The Threefold Cord

"The best marriage bond is this: two people committed to Christ and together committed to each other."

Ecclesiastes 4:12 (NIV): "Though one may be overpowered, two can defend themselves. A cord of three strands is not quickly broken." This verse illustrates the strength that comes from a marriage centered on Christ. The threefold cord, representing the husband, wife, and God, signifies a union that is strong and resilient.

In conclusion, premarital counseling provides couples with the tools and biblical principles needed to build a strong foundation for their marriage. By addressing potential issues, fostering open communication, and making spiritual commitments, couples can increase their chances of having a fulfilling and lasting marriage.

CHAPTER 38

Rape Recovery: Rescued and Restored

"Rescued and Restored" refers to the process of recovery and healing for survivors of rape and sexual assault. It involves a combination of physical, emotional, and psychological interventions aimed at helping survivors cope with the trauma of their experience and move toward healing and restoration. This may include medical treatment, counseling, therapy, support groups, and other forms of trauma-informed care. The goal is to empower survivors to regain a sense of control and autonomy over their lives and to help them rebuild their sense of self-worth and trust in others.

"The Lord is close to the brokenhearted and saves those who are crushed in spirit." (Psalm 34:18)

Understanding Rape and Its Impact

Men can also be victims of rape. However, the majority of rape and sexual assault victims are female. For the purpose of this discussion, I will refer to victims as female. Rape is defined as sexual intercourse by threat, force, or deception, victimizing males as well as females.

Statistics:

- 1 in every 6 women is sexually assaulted in her lifetime.

- Someone in the United States is sexually assaulted every 2 minutes.

- 7.7 million American women have been raped.

These statistics are even higher in some countries. If these statistics are accurate (and I believe they are conservative because so many rapes go unreported), you probably know a woman who has been raped.

Within God's heart, sex is an act of love.

Within a rapist's heart, sex is an act of violence.

Categories of Rape:

1. Mate Rape: Forced sexual relations by a husband.

2. Stranger Rape: Forced sexual intercourse by a person who is unknown to the victim.

3. Statutory Rape: Sexual intercourse with a minor, with or without force, when the victimizer is more than two years older than the victim. There is no such thing as consensual sex between an adult and a child.

4. Date/Acquaintance Rape: Nonconsensual sexual intercourse by people socially acquainted.

5. Gang/Group/Pack Rape: Sexual assault by two or more people, one of the most cruel and brutal crimes imaginable. (Judges 19:25)

Impact on Victims:

Rape is a heinous act that leaves lasting scars on its victims. It is incorrect to say that a wife must be subject to sexual relations with her husband at any time. The Bible teaches that marriage is a partnership based on mutual love and respect. (1 Corinthians 7:4)

Stages of Recovery:

Trauma Stage: Occurs within 2 days to 2 weeks after a rape. Symptoms include:

- Terror: Extreme fear causing flashbacks and nightmares.

- Refusal: Denial, causing memory loss or minimizing.

- Anger: Rage causing an inability to eat or sleep.

- Uncontrollable Actions: Feeling overwhelmed, causing hysteria and sobbing.

- Misplaced Guilt: Self-blame, causing nausea and diarrhea.

- Anxiety: Apprehension causing severe muscle tension and fatigue.

Scripture describes Tamar's pain following her attack by saying she "put ashes on her head and tore the ornamented robe she was wearing. She put her hand on her head and went away, weeping aloud as she went" (2 Samuel 13:19). The Bible also describes her long-term consequences: she "lived in her brother Absalom's house, a desolate woman" (verse 20).

The ABCs of Immediate Response to Rape:

1. ASSURE your own safety.

2. BEGIN a support system.

3. CALL on others for emotional support.

Rape victims find it incredibly difficult to talk about such a terrifying and painful experience. A counselor should provide a safe place for them to talk. Listen with understanding and compassion.

Walking Through the Season of Suffering: SUFFERING

- Seek God supernaturally to overcome the negative consequences of rape.

- Understand that no one is protected from tragedy.

- Forgive the offender and leave the revenge to God.

- Forgive others, family members, and friends who have let you down.

- Exchange your old identity for your new identity in the Person of Christ.

- Remember, the Lord is your Shepherd.

- Incorporate reading and meditating on Scripture along with listening to praise music as a daily habit.

- Notice and encourage others around you who are hurting. Your sensitivity and compassion for others will be a blessing to them and healing to you.

- Glorify Christ by allowing His splendor to be displayed through you.

Responding Appropriately to a Rape Survivor:

Galatians 6:2 (NIV): "Carry each other's burdens, and in this way, you will fulfill the law of Christ."

- Don't react with shock or horror, but respond with compassion.

- Don't suggest that the victim could have avoided it; affirm that the victim is not at fault in any way.

- Don't ask for details of the incident; suggest that the victim write down the details for authorities.

- Don't offer quick and simplistic answers; assure the victim of God's unfailing love.

- Don't press the victim to initiate immediate forgiveness; refer the individual for professional counseling.

- Don't infer that this was God's punishment for sin; encourage medical treatment.

- Don't change the subject; urge the victim to write down their feelings.

- Don't speak at all if you don't know what to say; comfort with your presence.

Affirm the future by holding out the hope that a return to normal living is possible. If the victim appears open to and ready for such a message, you may want to affirm that our God is a God who can make good come out of evil. Romans 8:28 (NIV): "And we know that in all things God works for the good of those who love him, who have been called according to his purpose."

CHAPTER 39

Reconciliation: Restoring Broken Relationship

Reconciliation refers to the process of mending a broken relationship or resolving a conflict between individuals or groups. It involves acknowledging past harms or wrongdoings, expressing remorse or apologies, and working towards forgiveness and mutual understanding. The goal of reconciliation is to create healing and closure, building stronger, more positive relationships based on respect, trust, and shared values. Reconciliation can occur on an individual, interpersonal, or societal level and may involve various approaches such as mediation, dialogue, and restorative justice.

"If it is possible, as far as it depends on you, live at peace with everyone." (Romans 12:18)

The Essence of Reconciliation

Reconciliation is the act of settling or restoring differences. It is a major theme of the New Testament and a common counseling issue. A mediator, an outside agent, is often brought in to facilitate change or compromise between opposing individuals. Mediation involves intervention between conflicting parties to promote reconciliation.

Initiating Reconciliation

The Bible instructs us to initiate reconciliation in two specific instances: when we have been wronged and when we have wronged another. (Matthew 5:23-24 and Matthew 18:15-16). The story of Joseph in Genesis 42-45 provides a profound example of reconciliation. Joseph reconciled with his brothers despite their severe sins against him but withheld reconciliation until they acknowledged their sin and demonstrated true remorse. Joseph's desire to be reunited with his family was strong, but he waited until his brothers showed genuine repentance, evidenced by changed attitudes, new desires, and self-sacrificing behavior.

Steps to Bury the Hatchet

To restore and reconcile relationships, one must prepare their heart and be willing to:

- Discover their own faults and risk the relationship.

- Expose their weaknesses and accept a potentially negative outcome.

God bore the penalty for the wrongs we did against Him. However, people often resist forgiveness unless the offender agrees to bear all the blame. In many conflicts, both sides share some fault. Each party should be willing to confess their part in the offense.

Humility in Reconciliation

Refusal to seek reconciliation affects one's intimacy with God. Therefore, one should humble their heart and pray:

- "Lord, help me not to be prideful."

- "Lord, I need Your favor on my life."

- "Lord, I want to reflect Your character when others look at me."

Seeking forgiveness and apologizing for hurtful words is crucial (Proverbs 6:2-3). Recognizing the ground rules of communication involves confronting the problem, not the person, and doing so with humility and gentleness (Ephesians 4:2). A godly approach to reconciliation reflects the character of Christ in all actions.

Handling Refused Reconciliation

If efforts for reconciliation are refused, one should:

- Remember that a repentant heart receives God's total forgiveness.

- Pray for those who refuse reconciliation, addressing their unmet needs.

- Control what is said about those who refuse to reconcile.

"Reconciliation is restoring a relationship based on restored trust. It requires repentance and is to be extended only when earned."

Living as Reconciled Saints

Romans 12:14-21 exemplifies living as reconciled and reconciling saints. We must extend our costly vertical reconciliation outward into costly horizontal reconciliation in two ways:

1. Blessing Persecutors: "Bless those who persecute you; bless and do not curse." (Romans 12:14). This reflects the character of Christ, who prayed for those who crucified Him (Luke 23:34).

2. Living in Harmony: "Live in harmony with one another. Do not be proud but be willing to associate with people of low position. Do not be conceited." (Romans 12:16). This promotes unity and peace, essential elements of reconciliation.

Reconciliation, at its core, is about restoring broken relationships with humility, grace, and a Christ-like attitude, fostering a community of love and trust.

CHAPTER 40

Rejection: Healing a Wounded Heart

"The Lord is close to the brokenhearted and saves those who are crushed in spirit." (Psalm 34:18)

Rejection is the act of refusing to accept or consider someone; it means being cast aside, cast off, or thrown away as having no value. When an individual grows up in a home where they feel that they never measured up, were mistreated, or misaligned, they are often convinced that God will never approve of them.

Understanding God's Promise

What promise from the Word of God can a counselor give a person who is thoroughly persuaded that God has rejected them? "The Lord will not reject His people; He will never forsake His inheritance" (Psalm 94:14). When an individual has been through the pain of rejection and feels that God does not approve of them, they need to understand:

- God's Character: "The Lord is compassionate and gracious, slow to anger, abounding in love" (Psalm 103:8).

- God's Heart: "For God so loved the world that He gave His one and only Son" (John 3:16).

- God's Plan: "For I know the plans I have for you," declares the Lord, "plans to prosper you and not to harm you, plans to give you hope and a future" (Jeremiah 29:11).

- God's Purposes: "And we know that in all things God works for the good of those who love Him, who have been called according to His purpose" (Romans 8:28).

Unless truth is embraced, the cycle broken, and the pattern replaced, rejection will continue to breed rejection.

The Tendencies of the Rejected

When a person has been rejected, they often tend to:

- Overgeneralize, assuming others will reject them as well.

- Fear the worst and push others away.

- Interpret negative reactions from others as rejection, confirming their deepest fears.

Counsel for the Rejected

What good counsel might the counselor offer an individual who has revealed feelings of rejection?

- Don't assume that one person's opinion reflects everyone's opinion.

- Don't let one person's attitude toward you define you.

- Realize that, because Jesus calls you friend (Luke 7:34), you can trust that His love will be with you always.

- Nurture several friendships, focusing on God's description of how true friends treat one another (Proverbs 17:17).

When an individual has been rejected or someone important to them withholds love from them, it doesn't mean everyone will withhold love from them. God always listens and never withholds His love (Psalm 66:20). When an individual has been rejected and someone important to them doesn't make them feel valued, it doesn't mean that no one values them. God valued them enough to send His Son to die for them, so that they might spend eternity with Him (John 3:16).

God-Given Needs

We are all created with three God-given inner needs—for love, significance, and security. Rejection begins when these needs are not met by someone important to us, depriving us of feeling loved, significant, or secure. Deuteronomy 31:8 reassures us that the Lord Himself goes before us and will be with us; He will never leave us nor forsake us.

When an individual realizes that they have been purchased with the priceless blood of Christ, that they are of utmost value to God and completely accepted by Him, they can find healing and triumphantly walk the road of transformation (Isaiah 42:16).

Focusing on Facts, Not Feelings

When dealing with issues of rejection, counselors should advise individuals to focus on the facts and not their feelings:

- Admit the rejection of the past and acknowledge its pain (Lamentations 3:19).

- Claim God's acceptance and unconditional love (Psalm 139:1-18).

- Choose to forgive those who rejected you (Colossians 3:13).

- Expect future rejection as a natural part of a fallen world (1 Peter 4:12).

- Plant scripture in your mind and produce new thought patterns (Romans 12:2).

- Thank God for what you have learned through the rejection (Psalm 119:71).

- Encourage others as an expression of Christ's love (Hebrews 3:13).

- Draw on the power of Christ's life within you (Philippians 4:13).

Path to Healing and Restoration

The way to find healing and restoration from the pain of rejection and feelings of worthlessness is by acknowledging that we must continue to put our faith in the fact that Christ gave His life for us, that He accepts us and will never leave us. Therefore, we must continue to allow Christ's leading by following in His footsteps, realizing that:

- Though I've been hurt, I will not harbor hate.
- Though betrayed, I will still live with love.
- Though my heart aches, I will still hold onto hope.
- Though I am afraid, I will face life with faith.

Embrace the promise of Psalm 34:18 and let God heal the wounds of rejection, restoring your heart and mind through His unfailing love.

CHAPTER 41

Salvation: The Cornerstone of Counseling

"For the Son of Man came to seek and to save those who are lost." (Luke 19:10)

The Need for Salvation

There are three crucial aspects from which we need to be saved:

- From the penalty of sin.

- From the power of sin.

- From the presence of sin.

The real problem we face is sin and guilt. That's the issue at the heart of humanity. God sent Jesus Christ to rescue us from the consequences of our sins, and everyone falls into the category of a sinner. It doesn't matter whether we're among the haves or the have-nots, whether we have great expectations or none at all, whether we're consumed by our passions or exhibit a degree of self-control and discipline—we are all sinners. We have broken God's law, and He is justifiably angry about it. Unless something changes our condition, we are on our way to eternal separation from God in hell. We need to be rescued from the consequences of our sins.

Assurance of Salvation

How do you know if you are saved? God wants you to be certain of your salvation, and He has devoted an entire book, 1 John, to help you know if you have eternal life. "I write these things to you who believe in the name of the Son of God so that you may know that you have eternal life" (1 John 5:13). The book of 1 John provides signs of authentic faith:

- "We know that we have come to know Him if we obey His commands" (1 John 2:3).

- "You know that everyone who does what is right is born of Him" (1 John 2:29).

- "Those who obey His commands live in Him, and He in them. And this is how we know that He lives in us: We know it by the Spirit He gave us" (1 John 3:24).

Many people attend church but are not sure if they are truly saved.

True Understanding of Salvation

any people understand salvation intellectually but never yield their will to God's will, allowing Him to take ownership of their lives. They continue to believe they can live a sinful lifestyle even after they are saved. We are saved by God's grace, not by our own will or works. Salvation is a gift from God and is irrevocable (Ephesians 2:8-9, Romans 11:29). If God has saved us, we are saved forever.

However, sinful actions committed as Christians will have consequences. On earth, we may face the loss of relationships, health, or freedom. Additionally, our actions will affect the level of rewards we receive in heaven. Our salvation is secure, but the quality of our eternal rewards depends on how we serve God while on earth (1 Corinthians 3:9-17).

Overcoming Doubts and Concerns

Some people have confusion and real concerns about whether salvation is even possible for them due to their awareness of their shortcomings and personal sins. The enemy, whose skill at deception and misdirection is unparalleled, uses feelings of unworthiness to lead us away from God's grace and love rather than toward Him. He is called "The Accuser," "The Father of Lies," and "The Adversary."

As a Christian counselor, how would you encourage those who question their salvation, thinking, "God could never forgive all my sins"? You would remind them that:

- God forgives all your sins if you repent and ask for His forgiveness (1 John 1:9).

- God forgets all your sins (Isaiah 43:25).

- God blots out all transgressions and remembers them no more (Hebrews 8:12).

The Bible records the guilt-ridden cries of many people throughout the ages who were crushed by the weight of their sins as they encountered a Holy God. Isaiah saw the glory of God as His presence filled the temple and cried out, "Woe to me, I am ruined! For I am a man of unclean lips, and I live among a people of unclean lips" (Isaiah 6:5). The Apostle Paul called himself "the worst of sinners" (1 Timothy 1:15). Yet, in spite of our unworthiness, our God continues to pursue us. The death of Jesus completely paid the penalty for our sins, and He freely offered forgiveness to all who put their trust in Him.

Decision for Christ

When someone says they don't want to make a decision for Christ right now, they have already made a decision—against Christ. But we should never give up hope. They could still make a decision for Christ, even on their deathbed. The most high-profile deathbed conversion in the Bible is the case of the criminal crucified alongside

Jesus (Luke 23:39-43). Only moments before his death, this criminal was an unbelieving mocker of Christ (Matthew 27:44). However, at the last moment, the criminal repented and acknowledged Jesus as the heavenly King. The Lord gave him the blessed promise, "Today you shall be with Me in Paradise."

However, many people die without having an extended amount of time to consider Christ. Many die instantly and unexpectedly, with no opportunity to trust in Christ. 2 Corinthians 6:2 declares, "In the time of my favor I heard you, and in the day of salvation I helped you. I tell you, now is the time of God's favor, now is the day of salvation."

Leading Someone to the Lord

What might the counselor say in leading someone to the Lord?

- God's purpose for you is salvation: "For God so loved the world that He gave His one and only Son, that whoever believes in Him shall not perish but have eternal life" (John 3:16).

- Your problem is sin: "If anyone, then, knows the good they ought to do and doesn't do it, it is sin for them" (James 4:17).

- God's provision is the Savior: "But God demonstrates His own love for us in this: While we were still sinners, Christ died for us" (Romans 5:8).

- Your part is surrender: "For it is by grace you have been saved, through faith—and this is not from yourselves, it is the gift of God" (Ephesians 2:8).

"I tell you the truth, whoever hears My word and believes Him who sent me has eternal life and will not be condemned; he has crossed over from death to life" (John 5:24).

As you share your personal testimony, you will encounter people who struggle with doubts over their salvation, who are plagued by this question, and who wrestle with it daily. Pray with them, and then share these verses to reaffirm God's promise of salvation:

- John 3:16: "For God so loved the world that He gave His one and only Son, that whoever believes in Him shall not perish but have eternal life."

- John 20:31: "But these are written that you may believe that Jesus is the Messiah, the Son of God, and that by believing you may have life in His name."

- Acts 16:31: "They replied, 'Believe in the Lord Jesus, and you will be saved—you and your household.'"

- Romans 10:9: "If you declare with your mouth, 'Jesus is Lord,' and believe in your heart that God raised Him from the dead, you will be saved."

- Romans 10:13: "Everyone who calls on the name of the Lord will be saved."

- Ephesians 2:8-9: "For it is by grace you have been saved, through faith—and this is not from yourselves, it is the gift of God—not by works, so that no one can boast."

- Titus 1:2: "In the hope of eternal life, which God, who does not lie, promised before the beginning of time."

- Titus 3:5: "He saved us, not because of righteous things we had done, but because of His mercy."

- 1 John 4:15: "If anyone acknowledges that Jesus is the Son of God, God lives in them and they in God."

- 1 John 5:13: "I write these things to you who believe in the name of the Son of God so that you may know that you have eternal life."

Salvation is the cornerstone of our faith and the foundation of all Christian counseling. Through Christ, we are saved from sin's penalty, power, and presence. By understanding and accepting this, we can live a life of assurance, hope, and eternal joy.

CHAPTER 42

Self-Worth: Discovering Your God-Given Worth

"The Lord does not look at the things man looks at. Man looks at the outward appearance, but the Lord looks at the heart." (1 Samuel 16:7)

Understanding Self-Worth

To have self-worth is to believe your life has value and significance. There are two different meanings for self-esteem:

- An objective regard of your value rooted in the recognition of your sin and your need for salvation.

- An exaggerated regard of your value rooted in the idea that you are good enough and sufficient within yourself, negating the need for dependence on the Savior.

Too often, we base our self-worth on how others see us, on our accomplishments, on shame from our past, on our looks, or by setting unrealistic standards for ourselves. But it doesn't have to be this way. If only we could see ourselves as God sees us! The true authority on our self-worth is Jesus Christ. Since He gave His life for us by dying on the cross, that should tell us just how valuable we really are.

Steps to Self-Acceptance

1. Accept God's Word that you were created in His image. (Genesis 1:27)

2. Accept yourself as acceptable to Christ. (Romans 15:7)

3. Accept the things you cannot change about yourself. (Romans 9:20-21)

4. Accept the fact that you will make mistakes. (Philippians 3:12)

5. Accept criticism and take responsibility for failure. (Psalm 32:5)

6. Accept that you will not be liked or loved by everyone. (John 15:18, 20)

7. Accept the unchangeable circumstances in your life. (Philippians 4:11)

Recognizing Your Worth in God's Eyes

The Bible has several passages that tell us what God has to say about our worth:

- Genesis 1:26-27: We are made in God's image.

- Psalm 139:13-16: We are fearfully and wonderfully made.

- Ephesians 1:4: God chose us before the foundation of the earth.

- Ephesians 1:13-14: We are God's own possession and have an inheritance in heaven.

Shaping Self-Image

A person's self-image is shaped by:

- Messages received and internalized from others.

- Our self-talk.

To align your self-image with God's image of you, consider the following steps to see yourself as God sees you, and help you on your road to transformation:

1. Accept yourself. (Proverbs 19:21)

2. Thank God for encouraging you. (2 Thessalonians 2:16-17)

3. Release past negative experiences and focus on a positive future. (Philippians 2:13)

4. Live in God's forgiveness. (1 John 3:2-3)

5. Benefit from mistakes. (Romans 8:28)

6. Form supportive, positive relationships. (Proverbs 13:20)

One of the best places to find a healthy support system is to get connected in a local church. Amazing things happen when people dedicated to their faith come together, trusting that God is available to help any who call upon Him.

7. Celebrate each accomplishment. (Deuteronomy 12:7)

Biblical Responses to Self-Defeating Statements

When struggling with low self-esteem, people often hear a critical voice within. Replace those negative thoughts with God's words of love and acceptance:

1. You say, "I just can't do anything right." The Lord says, "I will give you my strength to do what is right." (Philippians 4:13)

2. You say, "I feel I'm not able to measure up." The Lord says, "My power is perfect when you are weak." (2 Corinthians 9:8)

3. You say, "I don't feel that anyone loves me." The Lord says, "I have loved you with an everlasting love." (Jeremiah 31:3)

4. You say, "I feel my future is hopeless." The Lord says, "I know the plans I have for you, plans to prosper you and not to harm you, plans to give you hope and a future." (Jeremiah 29:11)

Embracing God's Truth

People with low self-esteem are often very critical of themselves, feeling inadequate, inferior, and incompetent. They need to catch themselves in the act of self-critical talk and replace those negative thoughts with God's words. Philippians 4:8 encourages us: "Finally, brethren, whatsoever things are true, whatsoever things are honest, whatsoever things are just, whatsoever things are pure, whatsoever things are lovely, whatsoever things are of good report; if there be any virtue, and if there be any praise, think on these things."

By embracing God's truth about our worth and focusing on His love and acceptance, we can overcome feelings of inadequacy and discover our true value in Him.

CHAPTER 43

Sexual Addiction: The Way Out of the Web

"Put to death, therefore, whatever belongs to your earthly nature; sexual immorality, impurity, lust, evil desires, and greed, which is idolatry." (Colossians 3:5)

Understanding Sexual Addiction

Sexual addiction is a compulsive, enslaving dependence on erotic excitement that results in detrimental patterns of thinking and behavior. It is now recognized as a psychological disorder similar to other obsessive-compulsive disorders or addictions such as alcoholism or illicit drug use. Previously, promiscuous individuals were simply labeled as immoral and filled with lust. Today, the issue is that what the Bible calls sin—promiscuous sex outside of marriage—is being rebranded as a psychological disorder.

Identifying Sexual Addiction

How can one know if they have a sexual addiction? If the answer to these questions is "yes," then the result will be revealing:

- Is the sexual activity secretive and not within godly boundaries? If yes, then you are living a double life.

- Is the sexual activity hollow and not a passionate relationship with your spouse, but empty sex? If yes, then you are prioritizing sexual passion over people.

- Is the sexual activity abusive and not uplifting to yourself or others, but degrading to both? If yes, then you are exploiting others and debasing yourself.

- Is the sexual activity mood-altering and not facing difficult feelings, but seeking an emotional quick fix? If yes, then you are using sexual passion for comfort or to avoid working through your pain.

- Is the sexual activity essential and not an option, suggesting you cannot live without sexual passion? If yes, then you are convincing yourself that sex is the most important thing in life.

Sin itself is addicting. Most sins, if engaged in regularly, can become habitual. Lying, drinking in excess, gluttony, rage, pornography, illegal drug use—all can become addictions. Ultimately, all of us, in our fallen bodies, have a sin addiction.

The Spiral of Sexual Addiction

The "Spiral of Sexual Addiction" follows this destructive path:

- Curiosity: A seemingly harmless temptation to look at sexual objects (James 1:14).

- Addiction: A recurring stimulus in the brain (Galatians 6:7).

- Compulsive Masturbation: A response of sexual self-comfort to relieve emotional discomfort (1 Corinthians 6:12).

- Escalation: The need for more shocking and explicit sexuality to be stimulated (Ephesians 4:19).

- Desensitization: The shocking becomes acceptable and no longer stimulating (Jeremiah 6:15).

- Acting Out: A compulsion to act out what has been seen or imagined because the visual experience is no longer satisfying in itself (Galatians 5:19).

- Despair: Utter disgust over the behavior and utter hopelessness to change (Romans 7:15).

Immoral sex, like other sins, can lead to "ever-increasing wickedness" (Romans 6:19). Just as drug use leads to increasingly potent amounts needed to achieve the same high, immoral sex can lead to increasingly frequent and wild intercourse to achieve the same satisfaction. We should never minimize the powerful hold sex addiction can have on a person. As with all sin addictions, the only true cure for sex addiction is Jesus Christ.

The Sequence of Sexual Addiction

Sexual addiction often follows this sequence:

- Sexual Fixation: A trancelike state where obsessing on sex becomes a sedative.

- Sexual Compulsion: Ritualistic routines heighten excitement, intensifying arousal.

- Sexual Gratification: A loss of self-control where the addict commits the sex act.

- Self-Condemnation: After the sex act, self-loathing occurs, and the addict recommits another sex act in attempts for relief, continuing the cycle.

Addressing Faulty Beliefs

The mind of the sexual addict is locked by faulty beliefs about their value, relationships, and sexuality. Reprogramming the addict's mind with the "right code" involves replacing these faulty beliefs with the truth and praying for God to open their heart. Encourage them to practice reading the following life-changing "True Beliefs":

- Your need for LOVE: False Belief: "I'm unlovable. Sex gives me a feeling of being loved." True Belief: You are loved. God loves you. (John 3:16; 1 John 3:1)

- Your need for SIGNIFICANCE: False Belief: "I'm unworthy. Sex makes me feel significant." True Belief: You already have worth; God has established your worth. (Psalm 139:13; Colossians 1:27)

- Your need for SECURITY: False Belief: "I'm unwanted. Sex numbs the pain of my insecurity." True Belief: You are wanted; The Lord wants you. (Hebrews 13:5)

The Doorway Out of Addiction

- Decide you really want to be set free. (1 Peter 1:13)

- Dispel the myth that you don't need help. (Psalm 51:10)

- Deal with the secret of child abuse. (Matthew 18:15-16)

- Discern the inner need you have tried to satisfy through sexual passion. (Psalm 51:6)

- Determine to let Jesus meet your needs. (Philippians 4:19)

- Dedicate your life to the Lord Jesus Christ.

This is a spiritual battle, and the biggest weapon in combating such an addiction is to come under the authority of Jesus Christ. If the sex addict is not yet a Christian, you should lead this person to totally surrender his/her life to Him and accept His gift of eternal salvation for his/her soul. After accepting Christ, many are totally delivered from their addictions.

The Pathway to PURITY

- Participate in an accountability group dealing with sex addictions.

- Uphold boundary lines that must be off-limits.

- Rid yourself, your home, and your workplace of all sexually addictive items.

- Incorporate the power of Christ daily when temptation overwhelms you.

- Take on positive habits of discipline, such as exercise, sports, regular sleep, and new hobbies.

- Yield your mind to meditating on and memorizing Scripture.

The Lord will never tell you to stop lusting without giving you the power to stop. God can make sex addicts a new creation (2 Corinthians 5:17) and begin the process of conforming them to His will (Romans 12:1-2), including enabling them to overcome sin and break any sin addictions they have. "Wretched man that I am! Who will deliver me from this body of death? Thanks be to God through Jesus Christ our Lord" (Romans 7:24-25).

CHAPTER 44

Sexual Integrity: Balancing Passion with Purity

"Whoever walks in integrity walks securely, but whoever takes crooked paths will be found out." (Proverbs 10:9)

Understanding Integrity

Integrity means being whole, undivided, and void of hypocrisy (Proverbs 11:3). The dictionary defines integrity as "a firm adherence to a code of especially moral or artistic values, or incorruptibility; incapable of being bribed or morally corrupted." In the Bible, the Hebrew word translated as "integrity" means "the condition of being without blemish, completeness, perfection, sincerity, soundness, uprightness, wholeness." In the New Testament, integrity means "honesty and adherence to a pattern of good works."

Defining Sexual Integrity

Sexual integrity is consistently living according to the highest moral sexual standards, consistently guarding your mind, will, and emotions from sexual impurities.

God's Blueprint for Healthy Sexuality

In Genesis 2, God lays out a blueprint for healthy sexuality that includes four key points:

1. Establishing a Family Unit Separate from Parents (Genesis 2:24): Marriage unites two individuals into a new single entity. This unity is described as "one flesh," emphasizing the sharing of all aspects—physical, emotional, intellectual, financial, and social. If a parent-child relationship overshadows the husband-wife relationship, it threatens marital unity, creating an unbiblical imbalance.

2. Cleaving to Each Other as the Priority Relationship (Genesis 2:24): The Hebrew word for "cleave" implies both pursuing and being glued to someone. A husband is to pursue his wife continuously and be "stuck to her like glue," indicating a relationship closer than any other, including those with friends or parents.

3. Sexual Relationship Begins After Marriage (Genesis 2:24): The "one flesh" relationship is reserved for the God-ordained marriage between husband and wife.

4. Openness and Vulnerability in Marriage (Genesis 2:25): Sexual and emotional intimacy in marriage should be marked by moral purity, honesty, and vulnerability, enhancing the bond between husband and wife.

Love vs. Lust

When infatuation turns to feverish passion, what seems like love often turns out to be lust—an illusion of true intimacy and a counterfeit of lasting love. Jesus warns against this in Matthew 5:28, teaching that even looking at someone lustfully is committing adultery in the heart.

- LUST is temporary; LOVE is enduring.

- LUST is selfish; LOVE is unselfish.

- LUST is uncontrolled desire; LOVE is controlled desire.

- LUST is based on fantasy; LOVE is based on reality.

- LUST focuses on external looks; LOVE focuses on internal character.

- LUST is eager to get; LOVE is eager to give.

Lust seeks to please oneself and often leads to actions without regard for consequences. In contrast, Christian love is marked by selflessness and holiness (Romans 6:19, 12:1-2; 1 Corinthians 6:19-20; Ephesians 1:4). Our goal must be to become more like Christ, putting off the old sinful nature and conforming to His standard.

Sexual Purity Outside of Marriage

God intended the sexual relationship for pleasure within the protected confines of marriage. Any sexual activity outside of a marriage between a man and a woman is never approved by God (1 Thessalonians 4:3). The question of "How far is too far?" should be guided by the following principles:

- Commitment: Never touch any part of another person's body covered by a bathing suit.

- Imagery: "Can a man scoop fire into his lap without his clothes being burned?" (Proverbs 6:27).

- Question: "Which steps can you take and still glorify God?"

- Scripture: "Among you there must not be even a hint of sexual immorality or any kind of impurity." (Ephesians 5:3)

While sinlessness is not attainable on earth, it remains our goal. In 1 Thessalonians 4:7-8, Paul emphasizes that God calls us to holiness, not uncleanness. If struggling with sexual impurity, confess it to God and seek His intervention.

Path to Sexual Purity

To combat sexual immorality and pursue purity of spirit, soul, and body, consider the following steps:

1. Write Out and Frame Your Vow of Purity (Ecclesiastes 5:4): Habakkuk 2:2 emphasizes the importance of writing down visions and goals. Making your vow known and permanent can help reinforce your commitment.

2. Find Like-minded Friends (Philippians 2:2): Abstaining from sex is easier with friends who share the same commitment.

3. Pray for an Accountability Partner (Proverbs 27:6): A trustworthy, honest, and courageous accountability partner can provide support and guidance.

4. Develop a Strategy for Countering Sexual Triggers (Proverbs 4:14): Avoid unfiltered internet access and other triggers that lead to temptation.

5. Make a List of Life Goals (Ephesians 2:10): Setting and working toward goals can help maintain focus and direction.

6. Wear a Purity Symbol (Psalm 61:8): A ring, bracelet, or necklace can serve as a constant reminder of your commitment.

7. Write a Love Letter to Your Future Spouse (Hebrews 13:4): This act can help reinforce your dedication to purity.

8. Rely on Church Teaching (1 Corinthians 6:13): Spiritual faith motivates righteous behavior.

Restoring Commitment to Purity

If someone has broken their commitment to sexual purity, they can take steps to restore it by embracing the acrostic I N T E G R I T Y:

- Invite others to walk the road of sexual integrity with you.

- Never put yourself or your loved one in tempting situations.

- Trust God to meet your need for love in the future.

- Enjoy others instead of using others.

- Give yourself only to sexually pure relationships.

- Refuse to justify any sexual impurity.

- Isolate yourself from tempting people.

- Transform your mind through the written Word of God.

- Yield to Christ, trusting Him to produce a life of purity in you.

Making a Promise List

Encourage individuals to make a Promise List, committing to:

- Practice sexual abstinence: Planting purity today reaps a harvest free from shame and guilt (1 Thessalonians 4:3).

- Date those committed to sexual integrity: Expect character, godliness, and sexual integrity.

- Set and maintain sexual boundaries: Focus on talk, not touch; conversation, not contact.

- Avoid compromising situations: Plan dates in advance to avoid gaps filled with temptation.

- Guard eyes, mind, and heart against impurity.

- Avoid substances that weaken defenses (Matthew 5:29-30).

- Avoid pornography and sex chat rooms: Remind yourself of the devastating consequences of sexual sin.

God forgives those who sincerely repent and take necessary steps to avoid temptation. Embrace the power of the Holy Spirit to live a life of sexual integrity, knowing that Christ empowers you to maintain purity.

CHAPTER 45

Singleness: How to Be Single and Satisfied

"I have learned to be content whatever the circumstances." (Philippians 4:11)

Understanding Singleness

Singleness is the state of a man or woman of marriageable age who is not married. This state can be categorized into three groups:

1. Single for All Seasons: Adults who never marry.

2. Single for a Season: Adults who will marry sometime in the future.

3. Single Again: The widowed, divorced, or separated.

Debunking Myths about Singleness

The myth that marriage is always the best option and singleness is second best is false. The truth is:

- Marriage is best for those whom God calls to marry.

- Singleness is best for those whom God calls to be single.

- Singleness, according to Scripture, is the best state in which to give all your attention to the Lord.

Our society often equates singleness with sexual immorality, which is very wrong. Paul promoted singleness so that a person could devote his or her full attention to the things of Christ. Singleness should never be used as an excuse to live in sexual sin. But if a single person can control their passions and live a morally pure life, there is no need to feel pressured to marry (1 Corinthians 7:37).

Contentment in God's Timing

God wants everyone to be content, whether single or married, as we patiently wait on His timing. It's always best to wait on God.

Consider the cautionary tale of Abram and Sarai (later Abraham and Sarah) in Genesis. God promised Abram a son, but rather than waiting for God to fulfill this promise, Abram and Sarai rushed things. Abram fathered a child with Sarai's servant, leading to much heartache. Sarah did eventually give birth to a son, but only after dealing with the consequences of not waiting on God.

God's timing is perfect. Waiting for Him to bring the right mate into our lives helps us avoid the heartache the rest of the world experiences when they look for love in all the wrong places.

God's Heart Regarding Singleness (1 Corinthians 7)

Singleness is a good state for widows. After experiencing the comforts of marriage, it can be tempting to settle for less than God's best. To avoid the temptation of settling, know what's acceptable and what's not, both to you and God, before you start looking for love. Spend time in the Word researching this.

Paul teaches in 1 Corinthians 7 that single people, especially those who are widowed, are often happier staying unmarried.

Challenges and Contentment

For many singles, there are moments and seasons of loneliness and longing — times when it feels awkward to be the only single person at the table or the party. Special moments that they long to share with another person can be challenging. But knowing that God has a good future planned for them can produce profound contentment in their present.

When a single person allows God to fulfill His purpose in their life, instead of pursuing their own, they begin on the Road to Transformation. 1 Timothy 6:6 says, "Godliness with contentment is great gain."

The Acrostic C O N T E N T

- C: Confess the difficulty. Admit your struggles and bring them before God.

- O: Overcome the "greener grass" mentality. Recognize the blessings in your current season.

- N: Nourish a heart of gratefulness. Regularly thank God for His provision.

- T: Treasure your identity in Christ. Find your worth and purpose in Him.

- E: Expect God to give you ministry. Look for ways to serve and bless others.

- N: Nurture a family of friends. Build strong, supportive relationships.

- T: Trust your future to God. Believe in His perfect plan for your life.

Living with Purpose

During a season of singleness, we have the opportunity to devote our time and energy to our relationship with God. We have more time to spend in prayer, Bible study, fellowship, volunteer work, and evangelism.

Bloom Where You Are Planted

Matthew 6:33 says, "Seek first the Kingdom of God and all these things will be given to you as well."

To ensure we are truly seeking God's kingdom first, we can ask ourselves: "Where do I primarily spend my energies? Where do I spend my money? Is all my time and money spent on goods and activities that will perish, or in the service of God—the results of which live on for eternity?"

Singles who have learned to truly put God first may rest in this holy dynamic: "... and all these things will be given to you as well." By focusing on God's kingdom and His righteousness, we find satisfaction and purpose in our singleness, trusting that He will provide all we need in His perfect timing.

CHAPTER 46

Stress Management: Beating Burnout Before It Beats You

"Come to Me, all you who are weary and burdened, and I will give you rest. Take My yoke upon you and learn from Me; for I am gentle and humble in heart, and you will find rest for your souls. For My yoke is easy and My burden is light." (Matthew 11:28-30)

Understanding Stress Management

Stress management refers to the set of techniques and strategies used to cope with and reduce the negative effects of stress on one's physical, emotional, and mental well-being. These techniques may include relaxation techniques such as deep breathing, mindfulness meditation, yoga, or tai chi, as well as physical exercise, healthy eating, and getting enough rest. Stress management may also involve cognitive strategies such as reframing negative thoughts, setting realistic goals, and practicing effective time management. Additionally, seeking support from family, friends, or a mental health professional can be helpful in managing stress. The goal of stress management is to reduce the impact of stress on one's life and improve overall health and well-being.

The Four Stages of Stress and Their Symptoms

1. Stage 1: NO Light - When there is "negative" demoralizing stress, a person avoids responsibility, has poor relationships, is unproductive, has no energy, experiences depression, has no purpose, and lacks perspective in life.

2. Stage 2: GREEN Light - When there is "positive" motivating stress, a person faces responsibility, has responsible relationships, is productive, energetic, enthusiastic, fulfills their purpose, and has a positive perspective.

3. Stage 3: YELLOW Light - When there is continual stress over a period of time, it will manifest itself in physical warning signs, like tension headaches, muscle aches, heavy sighing, high blood pressure, ulcers, hyper-alertness, loss of sleep/excessive sleep, lack of concentration, irritability.

4. Stage 4: RED Light - When stress is not processed, burnout occurs. Burnout leads to being overwhelmed by responsibility, withdrawal from relationships, minimal productivity, depression, purposelessness, fatigue, lack of concentration, indecisiveness, and irritability. This is not God's will for us.

While the Bible may not specifically use the word "stress," it speaks to anxiety, worry, and trouble, giving us clear answers on how we should deal with them. The dictionary defines stress as "physical, mental, or emotional strain or tension." Everyone experiences stress at one time or another, which can cause us to do things we would not normally do or cause us to shut down completely. Anything that causes stress is called a "stressor."

Signs of Burnout for the Overly Stressed Person
- Lower back pain and tension in the neck and shoulders.

- Trouble sleeping and feeling nervous and unsettled.

If an individual experiences four or more signs of burnout, they may need to evaluate how they are responding to the stress in their life and ask themselves if they are releasing their heavy load to the Lord and allowing His peace to permeate their hearts. (Proverbs 14:30)

Burnout is a state of emotional, physical, social, and spiritual exhaustion. It can lead to diminished health, social withdrawal, depression, and spiritual malaise. Jesus said, "Come to me, all you who are weary and burdened, and I will give you rest. Take my yoke upon you and learn from me, for I am gentle and humble in heart, and you will find rest for your souls. For my yoke is easy and my burden is light" (Matthew 11:28–30). The ultimate solution for those experiencing burnout is to find refreshment in Christ.

Adopting Healthy Stress Management Skills

By adopting healthy stress management skills, an individual can slow down, stop, yield, and resume speed at appropriate levels on their path of life and get out of the "Overload Ditch." 1 Thessalonians 5:24 gives God's peaceful assurance that He will never call you to do more than He gives you the time and ability to do. Paul and his companions were severely tested as they took the gospel into new areas. Paul testified, "We were pressed out of measure, above strength, insomuch that we despaired even of life. But we had the sentence of death in ourselves." (2 Corinthians 1:8–9). It sounds like Paul was stressed far beyond what he could bear. This fact leads us to another truth: our strength to endure stress, pressure, and temptation comes from God. Paul continued with praise to the Lord for His deliverance and emphasized the effectiveness of the prayers of the church (2 Corinthians 1:9-11).

Reevaluating Priorities and Seeking God's Peace

To make necessary changes to slow down and improve physical health, ask yourself: Am I getting adequate restful sleep most nights? If you need to reevaluate priorities:

- Make a list of everything you do and number them in order of importance.

- Eliminate unnecessary stressful obligations and don't accept impossible deadlines.

- Choose your commitments carefully and don't give in to the pressure of urgency.

Nourish your spiritual life by opening lines of honest communication with God about concerns and fears, setting aside time daily for personal prayer and Scripture meditation, and memorizing scriptures that build assurance of God's love.

Yielding to God's Sovereign Control

Yielding to God's sovereign control over your circumstances involves asking yourself:

- In what way(s) does God want me to change?

- Do I have pure motives or impure motives?

Adopting healthy stress management skills means slowing down, stopping, yielding, and resuming speed at appropriate levels on the path of life. Examine if you seek self-worth by proving your own adequacy and effectiveness, try to meet your own needs instead of waiting on the Lord, or look to people to accomplish what God can do.

Turning Away from Sin and Trusting in God's Provision

Keep stress from increasing by turning away from known sin and asking:

- Do I try to manipulate or control others?

- Do I overreact to criticism?

Disobedience and sin produce stress and cut us off from enjoying peace and joy. By obeying His commandments, we reap the blessing of a peace that passes all understanding (Philippians 4:7).

Living a More Peaceful Life

To decrease stress and live a more peaceful life, yield your rights and expectations to God. Many people become stressed because they don't trust God to provide for their needs. When we worry, we take the issue back into our own hands. When we trust God for provision, He brings opportunities to meet our needs right into our hands.

The Closing Charge

When stress signals a potential burnout, slow down and turn from danger, stop and ask for God's directions, yield the driver's seat to Christ, and resume speed, trusting in the Lord. Stress is a natural part of life (Job 5:7, 14:1; 1 Peter 4:12; 1 Corinthians 10:13). How we deal with it is up to us. If we choose to try to do it on our own, we face a long, uphill battle that will not end well. The only way to deal with stress is with Jesus Christ, first by believing in Him. Without believing and trusting in Him, we are on our own. We are "more than conquerors" in Christ (Romans 8:34). "Everyone born of God overcomes the world. This is the victory that has overcome the world, even our faith" (1 John 5:4).

CHAPTER 47

Suicide Prevention: Hope When Life Seems Hopeless

"Come to Me, all you who are weary and burdened, and I will give you rest. Take My yoke upon you and learn from Me; for I am gentle and humble in heart and you will find rest for your souls. For My yoke is easy and My burden is light." (Matthew 11:28-30)

"Hope When Life Seems Hopeless" is a message of suicide prevention that emphasizes the importance of providing hope and support to individuals who may be experiencing suicidal thoughts or feelings. Suicide prevention involves a range of interventions aimed at reducing the risk of suicide and promoting mental health and well-being. This may include crisis hotlines, counseling services, support groups, and mental health treatment. Additionally, suicide prevention efforts often focus on increasing public awareness and education around suicide risk factors and warning signs, and promoting effective communication and intervention strategies. The goal of suicide prevention is to help individuals feel valued, supported, and connected, and to provide them with the resources and tools they need to cope with life's challenges and move towards recovery.

God's Plan for Every Life

Suicide is never God's will for our life. He has a unique purpose and plan for each of us that validates our value and significance. The Bible mentions six specific people who committed suicide: Abimelech (Judges 9:54), Saul (1 Samuel 31:4), Saul's armor-bearer (1 Samuel 31:4–6), Ahithophel (2 Samuel 17:23), Zimri (1 Kings 16:18), and Judas (Matthew 27:5). Five of these men were noted for their wickedness (the exception is Saul's armor-bearer—nothing is said of his character). Some consider Samson's death an instance of suicide, because he knew his actions would lead to his death (Judges 16:26–31), but Samson's goal was to kill Philistines, not himself.

Recognizing the Signs of Suicide

Describe the successive signs and symptoms of a person contemplating suicide:

1. Early Stage: Downcast - Dejection, avoidance of family, anxiety, and boredom.

2. Advanced Stage: Distressed - Depression, rapid mood swings, self-pity, apathy. Suicidal intent is usually not related to one single cause factor. Rather, it is the overflow of a number of unresolved problems.

3. Danger Stage: Despairing - Hopelessness, deep remorse, previous suicide attempts or threats of suicide, organizing personal affairs, making a Will.

We have other examples of people in Scripture who felt deep despair in life. Solomon, in his pursuit of pleasure, reached the point where he "hated life" (Ecclesiastes 2:17). Elijah was fearful and depressed and yearned for death (1 Kings 19:4). Jonah was so angry at God that he wished to die (Jonah 4:8). Even the apostle Paul and his missionary companions at one point "were under great pressure, far beyond our ability to endure, so that we despaired of life itself" (2 Corinthians 1:8). However, none of these men committed suicide. Solomon learned to "fear God and keep his commandments, for this is the duty of all mankind" (Ecclesiastes 12:13). Elijah was comforted by an angel, allowed to rest, and given a new commission. Jonah received admonition and rebuke from God. Paul learned that, although the pressure he faced was beyond his ability to endure, the Lord can bear all things: "This happened that we might not rely on ourselves but on God, who raises the dead" (2 Corinthians 1:9).

Steps to Take When Suicidal Thoughts Arise

Below is a list of a few of the things a biblical counselor could suggest to an individual when suicidal thoughts begin to overtake them:

1. Pray: Psalm 31:1-3, Prayer verses 1-9; 14-24.

2. Recite Scriptures aloud: Psalm 57:1, also read Psalm 27 and 28.

3. Claim God's promise: Psalm 119:50.

4. Listen to Christian Praise Music and Scripture songs: Psalm 30:4-5.

5. Consider how special it is to be a child of God: 1 John 3:1.

People who are thinking about suicide will usually not try to hide it from others. You just need to be willing to ask. Talking to someone about their suicidal intent will not encourage them to attempt suicide. Instead, it typically communicates interest and hope because you cared enough to ask. Trust God to use you as His Instrument of Hope for someone who needs help!

Ensuring Safety in a Crisis

If the individual is still in crisis after taking these steps, to ensure their physical and emotional safety, they should get themselves to a safe environment in which they are not alone and:

1. Make arrangements to get together with a friend or supportive person.

2. Go to a public place where harming oneself is difficult.

3. If all else fails, go to a hospital emergency room and tell the staff that you are at risk for harming yourself and that you do not want to check in, but just sit in the waiting room. Have hospital staff sit with you or speak with a chaplain.

Even if an individual does not want to live, all they need is a willingness to be made willing. God can use the tiniest thread of hope to pull them out of the ditch of despair. (Psalm 51:12) When an individual is in the ditch of despair, yet has the willingness to be made willing, their attitude when asking the Lord to make them willing should be broken and yielded.

Confronting and Offering Hope

You extend hope to the hopeless by honestly confronting and:

1. Taking all talk of death seriously.

2. Asking direct questions such as, "Are you thinking about suicide?"

The Bible is a powerful example of suicide prevention. Acts 16 talks about when Paul and Silas were in prison in Philippi. When an earthquake opened the doors of the prison, the Philippian jailer drew his sword and was about to kill himself. He thought that the prisoners had all escaped, and he decided to kill himself rather than face execution. But Paul cried out, "Don't harm yourself! We are all here!" He intervened in the jailer's life and stopped him from killing himself. He gave him a reason to live and led the jailer and his whole family to Christ.

We can do the same. If you see people who are in despair, tell them, "Don't harm yourself! We are here for you!"

Offering Options and Communicating God's Purposes

You may also extend hope to the hopeless by offering options and:

1. Pointing out that choices in life often consist of unpleasant possibilities.

2. Listing possible options on a sheet of paper and ranking them in order of preference.

3. Communicating God's purposes for suffering.

The warning signs of suicide include prolonged depression and hopelessness, isolation or withdrawal, loss of interest in usual activities, giving away possessions, suicidal thoughts or fantasies, and suicide attempts. If you see these warning signs in a loved one, talk to them about it. Ask if they're doing okay, and specifically ask if they've thought about killing themselves.

Again - don't worry that asking someone about suicide might give them ideas. Many people who feel this hopeless are already thinking about suicide and desperately want someone to talk to about it.

Seeking Professional Help

You may also extend hope to the hopeless by:

1. Seeking a trained counselor or therapist, or a minister.

2. Contacting the Suicide Prevention Center.

The True Goal of Suicide Prevention

The true goal of suicide prevention is not the absence of life, but rather the absence of pain. By providing support, hope, and the message of God's love, we can help guide individuals out of the darkness and into the light of Christ's love and purpose for their lives. "For I know the plans I have for you," declares the Lord, "plans to prosper you and not to harm you, plans to give you hope and a future." (Jeremiah 29:11)

CHAPTER 48

Verbal and Emotional Abuse: Victory Over Abuse

"Are not five sparrows sold for two pennies? Yet not one of them is forgotten by God. Indeed, the very hairs of your head are all numbered. Don't be afraid; you are worth more than many sparrows." (Luke 12:6-7)

Understanding Verbal and Emotional Abuse

Verbal and emotional abuse are forms of abuse that involve the use of words, gestures, and behaviors to control, manipulate, and intimidate another person. Verbal abuse can include yelling, name-calling, insulting, criticizing, and blaming. Emotional abuse may involve actions such as isolating, ignoring, or withholding affection, gaslighting, and making the victim feel guilty or responsible for the abuser's actions. Verbal and emotional abuse can have serious negative effects on the victim's self-esteem, mental health, and overall well-being. It is crucial to recognize the signs of verbal and emotional abuse and seek help if you or someone you know is experiencing it. Counseling, therapy, and support groups can be vital in addressing the effects of verbal and emotional abuse and developing healthy coping strategies.

The Power of Words

Harmful words are words that hurt an individual, while helpful words are words that heal an individual. The Bible emphasizes the importance of speech in Ephesians 4:29: "Let no corrupt communication proceed out of your mouth, but that which is good to the use of edifying, that it may minister grace unto the hearers." The standards of speech for a Christian are extremely high. Abusive language of any sort should never pass their lips; rather, their speech should be instructive, encouraging, and uplifting, filled with thankfulness to God. The Christian's speech should act not only as a blessing to others but also as a purifying influence within society.

- Words that Hurt: Words that attack a person's identity, such as shouting or name-calling, can cause significant emotional damage. Proverbs 18:21 succinctly states, "The tongue has the power of life and death."

- Words that Heal: Words that address a person's actions, encouraging open discussion and casting a vision for the future, can promote healing and restoration.

The Impact of Abuse

Victims of abuse often experience a profound loss:

- Self-Worth: Increased self-consciousness and diminished confidence.

- Self-Perception: Increased self-criticism and a distorted self-image.

- Security: A heightened desire to escape their circumstances.

Over the long term, any kind of abuse can leave the victim feeling uncertain, unable to make decisions, and drained of any sense of personhood or value. The victim begins to accept the blame and believe the crushing words that are repeatedly thrown at them.

Confronting the Abuser

When confronting an abusive person, consider the following steps:

1. Educate Yourself: Understand the nature of abuse and its effects.

2. Set Boundaries: Clearly define what behavior you will not tolerate.

3. Seize the Moment: Address the abuse when it happens.

4. Surface Hostility: Gently bring the abuser's hostility to light.

5. Soften the Confrontation: Approach the abuser with a calm and gentle demeanor.

6. Stay in the Present: Focus on current issues rather than past grievances.

After establishing boundaries, communicate them clearly to the abuser. For instance, in a conversation or letter, state what you are willing to accept and not accept from the abuser (Proverbs 17:27). According to the Bible's definition of love, an emotional abuser should not be silently tolerated. Abuse dishonors the Lord and often escalates to physical abuse if left unchecked. Announce the consequences for violating your requests (Galatians 6:7), and enforce these consequences every single time abuse occurs (James 5:12). Seek support from wise, objective people (Proverbs 19:20).

Understanding the Abuser

Many abusers do not realize they are being abusive. If an individual answers 'yes' to three or more questions in the Honesty Test, chances are they are an abuser. The greatest need for an abuser is a desire to change (Psalm 139:23-24). The abuser will only find healing and forgiveness through genuine repentance and calling on the Lord. "Godly sorrow brings repentance that leads to salvation and leaves no regret, but worldly sorrow brings death." (2 Corinthians 7:10). The difference between godly grief and worldly grief is repentance.

Seeking Healing and Forgiveness

If an individual realizes they are an abuser, they must take responsibility for their actions. Believers need to own their abuse of others to break the cycle while receiving help to recover from past hurts. A safe place to do that is in pastoral or biblical counseling or in a small group of believers where people can help bear one another's burdens (Galatians 6:1-10). The Lord will enable us to do what He called us to do, which is to love one another as He loves us.

Verbal and emotional abuse can devastate individuals, but with God's guidance and the support of a caring community, victims can find healing and abusers can find redemption. "The Lord is close to the brokenhearted and saves those who are crushed in spirit." (Psalm 34:18). Through prayer, scripture, and the love of Christ, there is hope and victory over abuse.

CHAPTER 49

Victimization: Victory over the Victim Mentality

"It is for freedom that Christ has set us free. Stand firm then, and do not let yourselves be burdened again by a yoke of slavery." (Galatians 5:1)

Understanding Victimization

Victimization refers to the experience of being mistreated, abused, or subjected to injustice. This can profoundly impact a person's physical and mental health, self-worth, and ability to trust others. One of the most damaging consequences of victimization is the development of a victim mentality, a habitual way of thinking and behaving that keeps a person trapped in the role of a victim. This mentality manifests in feelings of powerlessness, blaming others for one's problems, and a lack of personal responsibility.

Breaking Free from a Victim Mentality

To overcome a victim mentality, it is crucial to recognize and challenge the negative beliefs and thinking patterns that keep you stuck in that role. This process may involve seeking therapy or counseling, practicing self-care and self-compassion, and developing a growth mindset that emphasizes personal agency and responsibility. Surrounding yourself with positive role models and building a supportive network of friends and family can provide encouragement and validation. Ultimately, victory over the victim mentality requires a commitment to self-reflection, growth, and the belief that you have the power to create a better life for yourself.

Understanding Victimization in Biblical Context

Victimization is defined in three ways:

- A person who is adversely treated

- A person who is tricked or duped

- A person who is injured, destroyed, or sacrificed

We find examples of this in the Bible: Abigail was married to an emotionally abusive husband, Nabal, described as "surly and mean" (1 Samuel 25:3, 14, 25). King Saul verbally mistreated his son Jonathan (1 Samuel 20:30). The Babylonians killed Zedekiah's sons before his eyes and then blinded him, combining physical and emotional abuse (2 Kings 25:7). Delilah's nagging of Samson until he was "sick to death" (Judges 16:16) is another example of emotional abuse.

The Victim Mentality

The victim mentality is a mindset where a person who was once a victim continues to feel powerless even after the victimization has ended. Romans 8:37 reminds us, "In all these things we are more than conquerors through him who loved us." People with a victim mentality often exhibit a poor-me attitude, avoid taking responsibility, and see themselves as helpless. They believe their unhappiness is always someone else's fault and demand rescuing from others.

God's Heart for the Victim

God deeply cares for those who have been victimized:

- God hears the cry of the battered and abused. (Psalm 10:17)

- God holds the victim of abuse in the palm of His hand. (Isaiah 41:10)

- God confirms the victim's value and worth. (Luke 12:6-7)

- God brings good out of the evil deeds of others. (Proverbs 16:4)

The Aftermath of Victimization

Victims often develop unhealthy beliefs and behaviors, manifesting in low self-esteem, which can be seen in individuals who:

- Accept abuse, blame, condemnation, and injustice

- Desperately seek approval

- Are unable to accept compliments

- Become people-pleasers

- Criticize themselves and others

Steps to Overcome Victimization

Those who have been victimized can take several steps to break free from a victim mentality:

- Recognize God's love: Ask God to reveal His love for you.

- Accept victimization: Acknowledge the reality of the victimization and release the desire for personal justice, knowing that God is the ultimate avenger (Deuteronomy 32:35; Romans 12:19).

- Confess anger towards God: Be honest about any resentment held against God and seek His forgiveness.

- Take responsibility: Decide to stop the cycle of wrong thinking and blame, looking forward with hope.

Addressing Misbeliefs about God

Victims often have a distorted view of God, fearing abandonment, intimacy, and rejection. Fearfulness is not designed by God. "For God has not given us a spirit of fear, but of power and of love and of a sound mind" (2 Timothy 1:7). Overcoming this spirit of fear requires trusting in God's perfect love, which drives out fear (1 John 4:18).

Physical and Spiritual Side Effects of Victimization

Victimization can lead to:

- Physical side effects: Sexual difficulties, sleeping disruptions, eating disorders, memory disturbances

- Spiritual side effects: Warped perceptions of God, anger at God, distrust of God, feelings of rejection and unworthiness, fear of God's anger and displeasure

Breaking Free from a Victim Mindset

To break free from a victim mindset:

- Accept yourself: Stop striving for perfection and accept yourself as you are (Proverbs 19:21).

- Acknowledge and praise God: Recognize and thank God for your abilities and achievements (2 Thessalonians 2:16-17).

- Release the past: Focus on a positive future, knowing that God is working in you (Philippians 2:13).

- Live in God's forgiveness: Embrace God's forgiveness and extend it to yourself (1 John 3:2-3).

- Benefit from mistakes: Trust that God works all things together for good (Romans 8:28).

- Form supportive relationships: Surround yourself with positive, supportive people (Proverbs 13:20).

Recognizing a Victim Mentality

Characteristics of a person with a victim mentality include:

- A need to justify themselves to others

- Constant self-comparison and self-pity

- Blaming others and not taking responsibility

- Seeking sympathy and validation from others

- Low self-esteem and self-worth

Recognizing and addressing a victim mentality is crucial for healing and transformation. By following the example of Jesus, who was kind to the unthankful and evil (Luke 6:35), and embracing God's love and forgiveness, individuals can break free from the chains of victimization and walk in victory.

CHAPTER 50

Worry: The Joy Stealer

"Do not be anxious about anything, but in everything, by prayer and petition, with thanksgiving, present your requests to God." (Philippians 4:6-7)

Understanding Worry

Worry can be defined as a state of anxiety or unease about an upcoming event or situation, often accompanied by obsessive thoughts or concerns. While some degree of worry can be normal and even helpful, excessive worry becomes a joy stealer, robbing individuals of their sense of happiness and contentment. When worry becomes chronic, it interferes with daily life, making it difficult to concentrate, sleep, or enjoy leisure activities. It can lead to physical symptoms such as headaches, muscle tension, and digestive problems. In severe cases, chronic worry can contribute to anxiety disorders or depression.

The Dangers of Chronic Worry

Chronic worry is detrimental not only to our mental well-being but also to our physical health. It disrupts sleep, appetite, and lifestyle habits, and it can lead to harmful coping mechanisms such as overeating, smoking, or substance abuse. Chronic worry can suppress the immune system, cause digestive disorders, increase muscle tension, and lead to heart problems. It is clear that worry, left unchecked, can wreak havoc on our lives.

Biblical Perspective on Worry

Is worry a sin? Worry can keep us stuck in a ditch of doubt and is therefore displeasing to God. The Bible clearly teaches that Christians are not to worry. In Philippians 4:6, we are commanded, "Do not be anxious about anything, but in everything, by prayer and petition, with thanksgiving, present your requests to God." We should bring all our needs and concerns to God in prayer rather than worry about them. Jesus encourages us to avoid worrying about our physical needs like clothing and food, assuring us that our heavenly Father will take care of all our needs (Matthew 6:25-34). Therefore, we have no need to worry about anything.

The Sinfulness of Worry

Worry becomes sinful when it leads us into:

- Disbelief: Worry reveals a lack of trust in God's provision (Isaiah 58:11).

- Disobedience: Worry shows that we are taking on responsibilities that God has already promised to handle (Matthew 6:25-31,34).

- Destruction: Worry destroys our physical body, which is the temple of the Holy Spirit (1 Corinthians 6:19-20).

- Dishonor: Worry shifts the focus from God's sufficiency to our human insufficiency (Matthew 5:16).

Living Worry-Free

To live free from worry, we need to:

- Desire to be free from all that chokes out the will of God.

- Recognize God's presence in our lives.

- Eliminate worry-producing demands.

- See worry-producing situations as opportunities for character building.

- Expect the Lord to bring positive changes, even through failures.

- Cultivate contentment through prayer.

- Implant God's promises in our hearts.

- Thank God for what He is doing.

Practical Steps to Combat Worry

Worry is a hard habit to break, but we can take practical steps to combat it. Writing down worries and literally throwing them away can be a symbolic way to let go and let God take control. Over time, as we continue to cast our worries on God, we may find that our worry basket remains empty more often.

Helping Others Overcome Worry

If you are counseling a worrier, ask them to commit to the following daily practices for the next four weeks:

- Focus on living in the present, not the past or future. Worry doesn't change anything. Everything you worry about falls into two categories: things you can do something about, and things you can't. If you can do something about it, thank God and do it. If you can't, turn it over to God.

- Emulate godly examples.

- Perform at least one unexpected act of kindness each day.

- Believe God's promises. You have the peace of God surrounding you and the God of peace within you (Jeremiah 17:7-8).

Trusting in God's Provision

Worry is relative to our situations, and it's not easy to stop worrying. Our human eyes are limited and cannot see God working behind the scenes. But God is able to do immeasurably more than we can ask or imagine. If you struggle with worry, deal with it one day at a time. Just for today, let go and let God take care of things. Trust in Him and see what He will do for you.

Victory Over Worry

By taking these proactive steps and leaning on God's promises, we can overcome worry and reclaim our joy. Trust in the Lord with all your heart and lean not on your own understanding. In all your ways acknowledge Him, and He will make your paths straight (Proverbs 3:5-6). Let go of worry and embrace the peace that comes from trusting in God.

APPENDIX

Supplementary Analysis of Christian Counseling

The Foundation of Christian Counseling

Christian counseling is rooted in the belief that true healing and transformation come from God. The core objective is to align the counselee's life with Biblical principles, facilitating a deeper relationship with Jesus Christ. The counselor, therefore, acts as a conduit of God's love, wisdom, and guidance.

"For the Son of man came to seek and to save those who are lost." (Luke 19:10)

Core Aspects of Christian Counseling:

1. Biblical Truth: Christian counseling relies heavily on the teachings and principles found in the Bible. Scripture serves as the ultimate authority and guide for addressing the issues faced by counselees.

2. Prayer: Prayer is an integral part of the counseling process, inviting God's presence and guidance into the sessions.

3. Holy Spirit: The counselor depends on the Holy Spirit for wisdom, discernment, and insight into the heart of the counselee.

4. Church Community: Encouraging counselees to engage with their local church community provides additional support and accountability.

The Role of Scripture in Counseling

Scripture is the bedrock of Christian counseling. It offers timeless wisdom and practical guidance for life's challenges. Here are a few key Scriptures that underscore the principles of Christian counseling:

- Guidance and Wisdom: "Your word is a lamp for my feet, a light on my path." (Psalm 119:105)

- Comfort and Healing: "He heals the brokenhearted and binds up their wounds." (Psalm 147:3)

- Transformation: "Do not conform to the pattern of this world, but be transformed by the renewing of your mind." (Romans 12:2)

Key Counseling Areas and Biblical Approaches

1. Salvation and Assurance

Salvation is the cornerstone of Christian counseling. Assuring counselees of their salvation through faith in Jesus Christ is essential for their spiritual and emotional well-being.

"For it is by grace you have been saved, through faith—and this is not from yourselves, it is the gift of God." (Ephesians 2:8)

2. Self-Worth and Identity

Helping counselees understand their worth and identity in Christ is crucial. Many struggles stem from a lack of understanding of who they are in God's eyes.

"I praise you because I am fearfully and wonderfully made; your works are wonderful, I know that full well." (Psalm 139:14)

3. Worry and Anxiety

Addressing worry and anxiety involves teaching counselees to trust in God's provision and care.

"Cast all your anxiety on him because he cares for you." (1 Peter 5:7)

4. Forgiveness and Reconciliation

Forgiveness is a central theme in Christian counseling. Encouraging counselees to forgive others and seek reconciliation is vital for their spiritual health.

"Be kind and compassionate to one another, forgiving each other, just as in Christ God forgave you." (Ephesians 4:32)

Practical Steps in Christian Counseling

1. Assessment: Begin with an assessment to understand the counselee's spiritual, emotional, and physical state.

2. Goal Setting: Establish clear, achievable goals that align with Biblical principles.

3. Scriptural Guidance: Use relevant Scriptures to address specific issues and provide hope and direction.

4. Prayer and Reflection: Encourage regular prayer and reflection to deepen the counselee's relationship with God.

5. Accountability: Foster accountability through the church community and trusted relationships.

6. Continual Learning: Encourage counselees to study the Bible and apply its teachings to their lives.

The Power of Community

The church community plays a vital role in the healing process. Encouraging counselees to engage with their church provides a support system and fosters a sense of belonging.

"And let us consider how we may spur one another on toward love and good deeds, not giving up meeting together, as some are in the habit of doing, but encouraging one another—and all the more as you see the Day approaching." (Hebrews 10:24-25)

Conclusion

Christian counseling is not just about addressing immediate issues but guiding individuals toward a transformative relationship with Jesus Christ. By grounding the counseling process in Biblical truth, prayer, and the power of the Holy Spirit, Christian counselors can offer hope, healing, and lasting change.

"Come to me, all you who are weary and burdened, and I will give you rest." (Matthew 11:28)

This supplementary analysis emphasizes the importance of Biblical principles and the power of God's presence in the counseling process, encouraging both counselors and counselees to trust in the Lord's provision and guidance for a fulfilling and victorious life.

BIBLIOGRAPHY

Primary Sources

1. The Holy Bible
   - New International Version (NIV)
   - King James Version (KJV)
   - English Standard Version (ESV)
Secondary Sources
2. Books
   - Adams, Jay E. Competent to Counsel. Zondervan, 1970.
   - Collins, Gary R. Christian Counseling: A Comprehensive Guide. Thomas Nelson, 2007.
   - Cloud, Henry, and John Townsend. Boundaries: When to Say Yes, How to Say No to Take Control of Your Life. Zondervan, 1992.
   - Crabb, Larry. Effective Biblical Counseling. Zondervan, 1977.
   - LaHaye, Tim. How to Win Over Depression. Zondervan, 1996.
   - Parrott, Les. Counseling and Psychotherapy. Wadsworth Publishing, 2003.

- Stanford, Matthew. Grace for the Afflicted: A Clinical and Biblical Perspective on Mental Illness. InterVarsity Press, 2008.

3. Articles and Journals

- Balswick, Jack O., and Judith K. Balswick. "The Dual-Earner Couple and Marital Adjustment: A Review of Research." Journal of Marriage and Family, vol. 39, no. 2, 1977, pp. 449–456.

- Worthington, Everett L. "Religiously Oriented Psychotherapies." Journal of Consulting and Clinical Psychology, vol. 56, no. 3, 1988, pp. 466–472.

4. Websites and Online Resources

- American Association of Christian Counselors (AACC). "Resources for Christian Counselors." [AACC.org](https://www.aacc.net)

- Focus on the Family. "Christian Counseling Resources." [FocusOnTheFamily.com](https://www.focusonthefamily.com)

- GotQuestions.org. "What Does the Bible Say About Counseling?" [GotQuestions.org](https://www.gotquestions.org/Bible-counseling.html)

- Biblical Counseling Coalition. "Articles and Resources." [BiblicalCounselingCoalition.org](https://www.biblicalcounselingcoalition.org)

5. Counseling Manuals and Training Guides

- Narramore, Clyde M. The Psychology of Counseling. Zondervan, 1960.

- Wright, H. Norman. The Complete Guide to Crisis & Trauma Counseling: What to Do and Say When It Matters Most. Bethany House, 2011.

Tertiary Sources

6. Encyclopedias and Dictionaries

- Elwell, Walter A., ed. Evangelical Dictionary of Theology. Baker Academic, 2001.

- Douglas, J. D., ed. New Bible Dictionary. InterVarsity Press, 1996.

7. Concordances and Study Bibles

- NIV Study Bible. Zondervan, 2011.

- Strong, James. Strong's Exhaustive Concordance of the Bible. Hendrickson Publishers, 2009.

Personal Communications and Unpublished Works

8. Lectures and Sermons

- Stanley, Charles. "Handling Life's Pressures." Sermon, First Baptist Church of Atlanta, 2010.

- Graham, Billy. "Hope for the Troubled Heart." Lecture, Billy Graham Evangelistic Association, 2008.

9. Unpublished Theses and Dissertations

- Smith, John. "The Role of Faith in Overcoming Depression." Ph.D. dissertation, Liberty University, 2015.

This bibliography provides a comprehensive list of sources that offer a wealth of knowledge and guidance on Christian counseling, helping counselors and counselees alike to navigate life's challenges with Biblical wisdom and support.